Boulder Hiking Trails

Boulder
HIKING

The Best of the Plains, Foothills, and Mountains

Third Edition

Ruth Carol Cushman and Glenn Cushman

Photographs by Glenn Cushman

PRUETT PUBLISHING COMPANY
BOULDER, COLORADO

Printed in the United States

11 10 09 08 07 06 05 04 03 02   5 4 3 2 1

Library of Congress Cataloging-in-Publication Data

Cushman, Ruth Carol, 1937–
    Boulder hiking trails : the best of the plains, foothills, and mountains /
Ruth Carol Cushman and Glenn Cushman ; photographs by Glenn Cushman.—
3rd ed.
        p.   cm.
    Includes bibliographical references and index.
    ISBN 0-87108-928-9 (alk. paper)
        1. Hiking—Colorado—Boulder Region—Guidebooks. 2. Trails—Colorado—
Boulder Region—Guidebooks. 3. Boulder Region (Colo.)—Guidebooks.
I. Cushman, Glenn. II. Title.

GV199.42.C62 B6835 2002
917.88'63—dc21   2002021995

Maps by Glenn Cushman, Janet Moore, and Tony Moore
Cover and book design by Jody Chapel

To all who have walked and skied these trails with us

and who share our love of open spaces and wild places,

and to the memories of our parents,

Florence and E. J. Scheerer and Eula and Ford Cushman.

Contents

Preface

This book is intended chiefly for newcomers and visitors to the Boulder area. It describes an array of our favorite trails, ranging from short strolls to strenuous hikes. We hope old-timers will also find it useful because of the historical tidbits and the section on connections, which allows hikers to plan permutations on old familiar routes. We've also included a few trails that are not well known.

Mileage is given from the most convenient parking area and for one-way, not round-trip distance, unless otherwise specified. When possible, we've taken mileages from signs and maps. When this information was not available, we used a "map wheel" and measured the distance on a map. Elevations are from topographic maps. "Short distance" means too short to bother measuring, and is usually the equivalent of a couple of city blocks. A trail name or destination that appears in boldface type indicates a trail you might enjoy exploring further.

We have not given hiking hours required because so much depends on the weather, the condition of the hiker, the steepness and condition of the trail, and how much time is spent watching birds, butterflies, and flowers. As a general rule, figure on two miles an hour for moderate trails.

Rating the trails as to difficulty is also subjective. However, we have used the following guidelines: *easy* means three miles or less one way, with less than 1,000 feet elevation gain and gentle gradients; *moderate* means between three and four miles one way and less than 1,500 feet elevation gain; *strenuous* means either more than four miles one way, more than a 1,500-foot elevation gain, or a gradient of more than 1,000 feet per mile. Using these criteria, the Mallory Cave Trail, for example, is listed as strenuous even though it is very short. Experienced or strong hikers will find our ratings too easy.

The book is divided into three sections: Plains, Foothills, and Mountains. Within each section the trails are arranged roughly from north to south. We used USGS 7.5 minute series quadrangle maps for proper names and, consequently, have omitted apostrophes in such names as Longs Peak.

A warning to the reader: Trails, like living organisms, tend to change—sometimes very quickly. New trails are constructed, old trails are rerouted or closed, trail names are changed, old bridges collapse, and (sometimes) new bridges are built. So if you find outdated descriptions in our guide, please forgive us and realize that any outdoor adventure may involve coping with the unexpected.

A list of the "Best of the Best for . . . ," wheelchair-accessible trails, and suggestions for hiking ethics and safety are in the appendices, and there is a bibliography. For anyone interested in doing technical climbs in the Boulder area, we recommend Gerry Roach's guides, and for peak-baggers, we recommend Robert Ormes's classic *Guide to the Colorado Mountains*, both of which give more detailed routes than we provide in this book.

Acknowledgments

We would like to thank the following people for generously supplying information: Lois Anderton, David Bell, Jim Benedict, Terry Boone, Marta Bromschwig, Anne Dyni, Irby Downes, Dennis Fisher, Paula Fitzgerald, Pascale Fried, Ken Huson, Gary Lacy, Rich Lippincott, Dick Lyman, Joanna Sampson, Vi Schweiker, Dock Teegarden (the first volunteer for City Open Space), Pam Tierney, and Jim Weibel. The resources of the Boulder Carnegie Branch Library for local history and the University of Colorado libraries were invaluable.

Special thanks go to Stephen Jones for past collaborations, for ongoing encouragement, and for sharing his knowledge of the natural world, and to Betty Lane for faithfully keeping our weekly hiking date regardless of weather.

We are grateful to Peter Gleichman, Rich Koopmann, Mary McNellan, Martha Moran, John Oppenlander, and Brent Wheeler, who not only provided essential information but also critiqued portions of the manuscript. Any errors that appear here, however, are ours.

We used the revised USGS topographic maps as our main source for the trail maps, and we freehanded minor trail revisions. For trails that are more recent than the latest USGS revision, we relied on brochures published by various public agencies to supply information missing from the topos. The extensive trail net in the Boulder Mountain Parks and the Brainard Lake area presented a special case; we used the 1984 and 1993 Colorado Mountain Club maps as our prime source for trail locations in these areas, with thanks to Harlan Barton, Jim Groh, and the Boulder Group of the Colorado Mountain Club.

The book looks better than we could have imagined thanks to the skill of book designer Jody Chapel. And, of course, we couldn't have done it without Jim Pruett, who is an enthusiastic hiker and publisher, and Marykay Scott and Kim Adams, talented editors who are great at spotting errors and inconsistencies.

A Brief History of Hiking, Parks, and Open Space in the Boulder Area

Ever since the first white settlement in 1858, hiking and nature study have been popular activities in the Boulder area. When the first gold seekers camped at Red Rocks that year, some of them climbed the hill to observe the last rays of the sun illuminate what they called "Sunset Rock," possibly the edge-on view of the first flatiron. In the late 1860s and 1870s, Martha Maxwell—one of the first women naturalists in the country—explored the Boulder area on foot and horseback. It was here that she gathered specimens for the collection she exhibited, to worldwide acclaim, at the Philadelphia Centennial Exhibition in 1876.

Soon after Chautauqua was established in 1898, the Colorado Chautauqua Climbers Club was formed and later incorporated as the Rocky Mountain Climbers Club (RMCC). The articles of incorporation listed various objectives, including, "to mark, build, and establish and maintain trails to points of interest." Edwin Chamberlain, a charter member, wrote: "We had no trail in those days to Royal Arch, Green Mountain, nor Bear Peak. We just clambered around like mountain goats." Another group, "The High Hikers," also constructed trails throughout the county. This group was organized in 1910 and later became the Boulder Chapter of the Colorado Mountain Club. A. T. Wheeler, who patrolled on horseback, was hired in 1911 as the first Boulder Mountain Parks ranger. In 1916 M. R. Parsons, who also patrolled on horseback, was hired. Parsons's extensive photo collection is an important historic source for Boulder.

Today Boulder County is famous for its protected open spaces and trail systems. But when it was first settled, there was no need to set aside special parks—almost everything was "open space." Nevertheless, the original Boulder City town-site plan designated "The Public Square," the site of the present-day courthouse, as a park. In 1882, this park became the site for the courthouse, and Boulder had no municipal parks from 1882 to 1898. The Texas-Colorado Chautauqua popularized outdoor activities as well as cultural programs. Chautauqua was a "cultural retreat" with lectures, musical performances, and entertainment. The movement started in New York and spread to Boulder in 1898. Healthy living was emphasized and, as Boulder Chautauquans did a lot of hiking, there was a

1

growing demand for trails. In response to this demand, the Boulder City Coun-
cil purchased eighty acres on the east slope of Flagstaff Mountain in 1898 and
persuaded the U.S. government to grant the city additional land for a park.

Later, the city acquired public lands extending from Sunshine Canyon
to South Boulder Creek. Additional purchases have been made to the present day. The park system was also expanded by gifts from such individu-
als as Dr. and Mrs. William Baird, who donated 160 acres in Gregory
Canyon in 1908, and Charles Buckingham, an early Boulder banker, who
gave sites in Lefthand Canyon and at Boulder Falls.

Frederick Law Olmsted, Jr., a noted landscape architect, came out
from Harvard University in 1908 to advise on the beautification of the city.
He recommended burying all utility wires and that the city *not* be developed
for the benefit of tourists, who, he said, "hastily pass through a place which
attracts them . . . taking not the slightest interest in the welfare . . . of the
permanent residents."

Olmsted urged the city to commit the Boulder Creek floodplain to play-
ing fields and walkways: "If the matter is taken in hand now the city will
spend less money on the hydraulic improvement and get a beautiful park-
way to boot." Sixty some years later, when the city finally acted on his advice and started developing the Boulder Creek Path, many buildings had
already been built in the floodplain and some officials favored channelizing
the creek and lining it with concrete.

Boulder's Open Space Program, so popular today, began with the Blue
Line Ordinance passed by Boulder voters in 1959. The "Blue Line" is a
boundary at an elevation of about 5,750 feet, above which the city will not
provide water or sewer services. However, the ordinance did not protect
the mountain backdrop sufficiently. This became evident in 1960, when a
luxury hotel on Enchanted Mesa was proposed. "Save Enchanted Mesa"
became the rallying cry for a successful campaign to purchase most of the
mountain land, though some "unscenic" mansions have been and are still
being built on the mesa. In 1967, voters passed a small sales tax to be used
for "greenbelt" acquisition.

In recent years both Lafayette and Louisville have begun purchasing
open space, and most communities in Boulder County are adding parks and
building additional trails. In 1993, a county sales tax was passed by a large
majority of voters who hope to preserve what is left of our open spaces. In
1994 Boulder County made several large, important purchases, including
the Heil Ranch north of Lefthand Canyon, and the Hall Ranch, near Lyons.

In 2000 the City of Boulder Open Space and the Mountain Parks Departments merged. Their combined staffs will continue to acquire and main-

tain land to preserve habitat and to provide recreation. New problems and conflicts arise with our soaring population growth, however. Today we may be at the point of loving our trails and open space to death. Perhaps it is time to question whether every stream should have its trail and whether every trail can withstand all types of recreational use.

ABBREVIATIONS AND MAP LEGEND

CR—County Road
SR—State Road
US—United States Highway
FS—Forest Service
NCAR—National Center for Atmospheric Research
RMNP—Rocky Mountain National Park
USGS—United States Geological Survey

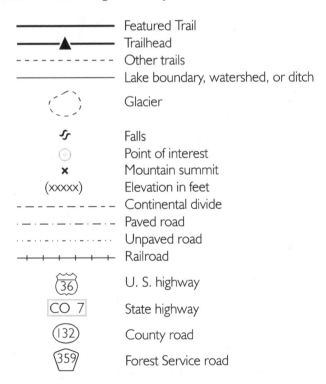

———————	Featured Trail
———▲———	Trailhead
- - - - - - - - -	Other trails
———————	Lake boundary, watershed, or ditch
( )	Glacier
ℐ	Falls
⊙	Point of interest
×	Mountain summit
(xxxxx)	Elevation in feet
- - - - - - - -	Continental divide
· — · — · — · — · ·	Paved road
· · · · · · · · · · · ·	Unpaved road
+—+—+—+—+—+	Railroad
(36)	U. S. highway
CO 7	State highway
(132)	County road
(359)	Forest Service road

 Note: Trailheads in maps may mark a trailhead, parking area, or campground. Some actual trails and trailheads may have no physical marker and are unnamed in our maps.

Plains

Subdivisions and shopping centers cover much of what was once prairie and, later, agricultural land in eastern Boulder County. However, we are lucky that some of this land has been purchased and preserved by various city and county open space departments. These organizations have developed most of the trails described in this section. Because many of the trails are relatively new, they may not be shown on USGS topographic maps. Although we have listed the appropriate topo maps, we recommend using the City of Boulder Open Space Map, available in area sporting goods stores and in open space department offices.

All of these clearly marked trails are easy, with little elevation change (most of them are between 5,100 and 5,500 feet in elevation), and can be hiked at any time of year. However, in summer they are more pleasant early or late in the day. They are also good for ski touring immediately after a heavy winter snowstorm.

St. Vrain Greenways Trail

Distance: 9 miles one way when completed
Elevation: 4,980 feet at Golden Ponds, with negligible elevation gain
Highlights: Ponds, birdwatching, fishing, mountain views
Difficulty: Easy
Topo maps: Hygiene, Longmont

Description

This paved trail along St. Vrain Creek in Longmont will eventually stretch from Golden Ponds, past the 313-acre Sandstone Ranch and community park, to the old city landfill east of Weld CR 1. At present, the three completed miles stretch from Golden Ponds to Main Street, with an attractive side loop around Fairgrounds Pond. Golden Ponds are restored gravel pits that attract a variety of birds and offer superb views of Longs Peak and Mount Meeker. Along the trail and near Rogers Grove look for the stone nature sculptures by artist Robert Tully. We especially love the one shaped like an ear, where you sit to hear the amplified sound of the creek.

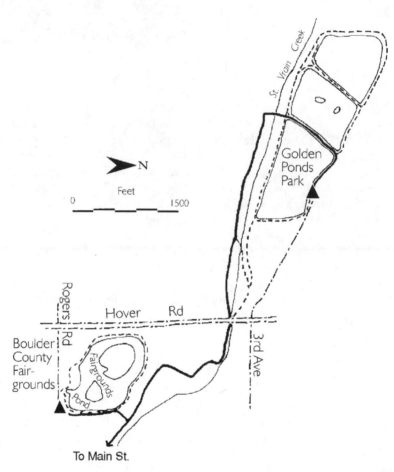

St. Vrain Greenways Trail

History

The St. Vrain River attracted the first farmers to its fertile valley in the 1860s, when Alonzo Allen and his stepson, William Henry Dickens, home-steaded on the south bank and founded the town of Burlington—the fore-runner of Longmont. A stone monument and plaque along the river west of Main Street marks the site of their original cabin.

A group of Chicago investors bought the land that is now Longmont in the 1870s. The Chicago-Colorado Colony created an agricultural commu-nity and built irrigation ditches to use St. Vrain River water for farming. In 1903, the Great Western Sugar Company built a factory on the east side of

Views along the St. Vrain Greenways Trail

town, and the sugar beet industry flourished. In early fall you can still glean sugar beets that have fallen from the trucks along the dirt roads east of town.

Access

In Longmont, turn west off Hover Road where Hover Road and 3rd Street intersect and park at Golden Ponds. Other trailheads begin at Fairgrounds Pond and Rogers Grove (east of Hover Road and 3rd Street) and at Izaak Walton Park (18 South Sunset Street).

Pella Crossing

Distance: 1-mile loop with spur to Webster Pond
Elevation: 5,097 feet with no elevation change
Highlights: Views of Longs Peak and Indian Peaks, water birds, fishing, picnicking
Difficulty: Easy
Topo map: Hygiene

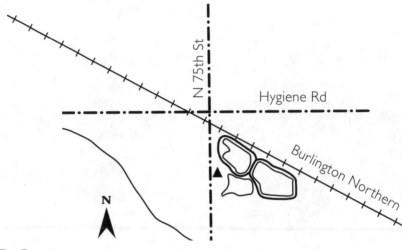

Pella Crossing

Description

A hard gravel trail loops around Sunset Pond and Heron Lake with a spur to Webster Pond. As you might guess from the names, great blue herons (and other water-loving birds) can be seen here, and the views at sunset are spectacular. Views are impressive at sunrise too. On a windless day at dawn, Longs Peak, bathed in alpenglow, is reflected in the lakes.

History

The first settlers, George Webster (for whom the pond is named) and Charles True, bought a 160-acre homestead claim here in 1859, and later, Webster planted plum, cherry, and apple orchards. In the 1860s the Overland Trail crossed the St. Vrain River at "Upper Crossing" (original name for Pella Crossing) on the route between Denver and Laramie. By 1861, Pella had become "one of the busiest towns north of Denver," according to the sign at the trailhead. The town even had a racetrack.

Connections

It is worth taking the paved path northwest of the ponds to see the historic town of Hygiene, shaded by enormous, spreading cottonwoods.

Canada geese on Heron Lake

Access

Head for the town of Hygiene. The Pella Crossing sign and parking lot are on North 75th Street, a half mile north of the intersection of 75th and St. Vrain Road, just south of Hygiene.

Coot Lake to Boulder Reservoir

Distance: 1 mile one way
Elevation: 5,173 feet with negligible elevation change
Highlights: Wetlands, waterbirds, wildflowers, prairie dogs, raptors, fishing, and mountain views
Difficulty: Easy
Topo map: Niwot

Description

This trail, a convenient hike from either direction, is especially beautiful at sunset and is a good place to watch the full moon rise. On the west

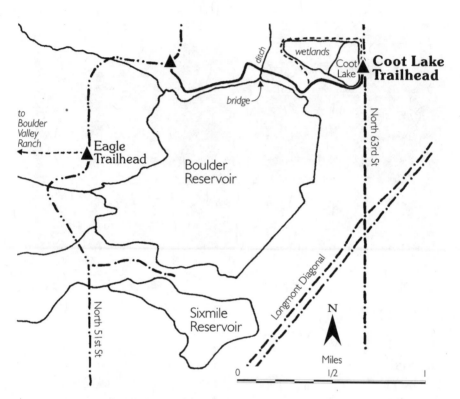

Coot Lake to Boulder Reservoir

end of Coot Lake a cattail marsh and several small ponds usually harbor ducks, red-winged blackbirds, and a northern harrier.

Skirt the south side of Coot Lake (turn left from parking lot) and join an old road. For a longer but more scenic route, you can skirt the north and west sides of the lake by turning right from the parking lot. Walk along this dirt road to a bridge across an irrigation canal. Cross the canal on this bridge and don't even think of dropping down into the ditch—signs warn of "certain death" for anyone sucked into the siphon draining the ditch! From the bridge, follow the trail through a prairie dog town and above the shore of Boulder Reservoir to 51st Street.

In early spring Easter daisies bloom here, followed by yucca, prickly pear cactus, various composites, and—finally—gayfeather in the fall. Prairie grasses, such as blue grama, and dried teasel heads remain decorative into

Coot Lake Wetlands

winter. Red-tailed hawks soar frequently over the prairie dog town, and bald eagles are sometimes seen in winter.

History

In 1902, a nearby oil boom was sometimes called the "Haystack Field" because of its proximity to Haystack Mountain, which rises out of the plains northwest of Coot Lake. It was predicted that a "sea of derricks" would stretch to the Wyoming border, but production peaked in 1909 and virtually ended by the mid-1920s. Coot Lake achieved notoriety during the 1970s and early 1980s as a nude swimming hole. Later, the city closed the area to swimming largely because of liability problems, and now it is chiefly a haven for waterbirds such as the coots for which it is named. (Nude bathers sometimes called themselves "cooties.") Boulder Reservoir was completed in February 1955, after nine months of construction. The dam is 1.2 miles long, 48 feet high, and 265 feet thick at the bottom. Water comes from Lake Granby on the Western Slope via the Big Thompson Project.

Connections

You can make a 6-mile loop around **Boulder Reservoir** by connecting trails and roads, but be careful of traffic. Half a mile north of the main entrance to Boulder Reservoir, you can cross the road to connect to the **Eagle Trail** and to the network of trails at **Boulder Valley Ranch** (see page 12).

Access

From the Diagonal Highway (SR 119) between Boulder and Longmont, turn west on CR 39 (for Coot Lake) or Jay Road (for Boulder Reservoir). On CR 39 drive 0.7-mile and park at Coot Lake. From Jay Road, turn right on 51st Street, drive 3.2 miles, and park at the northwest end of Boulder Reservoir.

Boulder Valley Ranch: Eagle Trail

Distance: 3.2 miles one way
Elevation: 5,230 to 5,533 feet
Highlights: Working ranch, wetlands, waterbirds, wildflowers, prairie dogs, raptors, and mountain views

Difficulty: Easy
Topo maps: Boulder, Niwot

Description

This trail connects 51st Street and US 36 and has numerous laterals and loops. Starting at the Eagle Trailhead on 51st Street, the trail heads west (with views of the Indian Peaks) for 0.5-mile to a fork, where **Sage Trail** goes right. Turn left and skirt the lower end of a shallow pond and walk past a prairie dog colony. Watch for raptors overhead, waterbirds in the pond, and great horned owls in the cottonwoods. In winter, both golden and bald eagles may be seen. In 1 mile the trail forks again, with another section of Sage going to the right, following Farmers Ditch. Take the left fork and head uphill to Mesa Reservoir. Once filled with irrigation water, this area has been dry since the 1970s and is now a wildlife habitat with several different species of trees filling the former reservoir. Continue following the signs for Eagle Trail to the **Foothills Trailhead** on US 36. Most of the trails in this area, which is still a working ranch, are actually farm access roads.

In spring and early summer the wildflowers (including evening primrose, cowboy's delight, and several species of mustard and penstemon) bloom extravagantly along the shale cliffs. Because there is little shade, this trail is best done off-season or early or late in the day during summer.

History

Farmers Irrigation Ditch, built in 1862, provided power for the Yount-McKenzie Flour Mill near the mouth of Boulder Canyon and has provided water to area farmers for more than a century. Around the turn of the century the earliest cattle ranchers in Boulder (W. W. Degge, W. W. Wolfe, Clinton Tyler, the Burger family, and the Maxwell family) sometimes ran cattle from here over Rollins Pass, to as far as Steamboat Springs to take advantage of the nutritious mountain grasses.

The adobe brick building at Boulder Valley Ranch was built in the early 1900s, and is one of the oldest buildings still in use at the ranch. Called the "Silver Nickel," this converted barn has been used over the years as a dance hall and a livery stable. Many of the trails at the ranch were created by early riders who stabled their horses here.

Connections

Eagle, Sage, Mesa Reservoir, Cobalt, Degge, and **Hidden Valley trails** make various loops and permutations throughout the ranch. **Left Hand Trail,** opened in 1999, connects Sage Trail to Neva Road, skirting

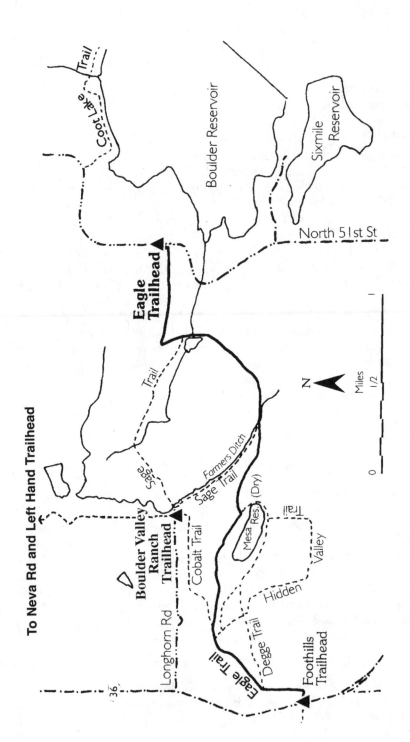

Boulder Valley Ranch: Eagle Trail

Boulder Valley Ranch: Eagle Trail

Lefthand Valley Reservoir and the Beech Open Space picnic pavilion. To connect with the trail to **Coot Lake,** turn left from the Eagle Trailhead parking area and walk 0.9 mile along the road; the trail skirts the north side of Boulder Reservoir. To connect with the **Foothills Trail** (see page 62), cross under the Foothills Highway at the Foothills Trailhead.

Access

Four trailheads give access to this area: Boulder Valley Ranch Trailhead on Longhorn Road, about 2 miles north of the intersection of US 36 and North Broadway and 1 mile east of US 36; Foothills Trailhead, 0.4-mile north of the intersection of US 36 and North Broadway on US 36; Eagle Trailhead, on the west side of 51st Street, half a mile north of the entrance gate to Boulder Reservoir; and Left Hand Trailhead on Neva Road, about 1.5 miles east of US 36.

East Boulder Trail: White Rocks and Gunbarrel Farm Sections

Distance: 4.5 miles one way
Elevation: 5,110 to 5,415 feet
Highlights: White Rocks Nature Preserve, mountain views, raptors (including bald eagles in winter), waterbirds on the lake and creeks, white-tailed and mule deer
Difficulty: Easy to moderate
Topo map: Niwot

Description

Starting at the Teller Farm North Trailhead, go west for a short distance, cross Valmont Road, and head north following Dry Creek (which isn't dry). Cross the railroad track and skirt the restored gravel pit (closed to the public), which provides habitat for many waterbirds. The trail circles east of the ponds, crosses Boulder Creek and an irrigation canal, climbs a couple of small ridges, and in 2.4 miles comes to a T-junction. Turn west and continue to the crest of Gunbarrel Hill, where views of the foothills and Indian Peaks are superb. Along the way watch for raptors, coyotes, and herds of white-tailed and mule deer.

This segment of the trail terminates at Boulderado and Cambridge Streets in the Heatherwood subdivision. You can continue on paved sidewalks to Lookout Road and 75th Street, however. Eventually, the trail may be extended north.

History

Native Americans inhabited this area in prehistoric times, and a few faint petroglyphs have been found as well as names of westering pioneers who traveled the creek corridor in the mid-1800s. The buff-colored sandstone formation northwest of the ponds is home to rare miner bees that drill into rocks, to *Asplenium adiantum-nigrum* (a fern found in only four other localities on this continent), and to nesting barn owls. For many years this unusual ecosystem was vigorously protected by private landowners such as Martha Weiser and the Tell Ertl family (who developed the Eldora Ski Area). Now, the City of Boulder permits only a limited number of researchers into the actual White Rocks area, which is fenced off from the trail and is a state-designated natural area.

Winter wheat was raised on Gunbarrel Hill from the early days until the mid-1980s, when the land was purchased by the City of Boulder Open

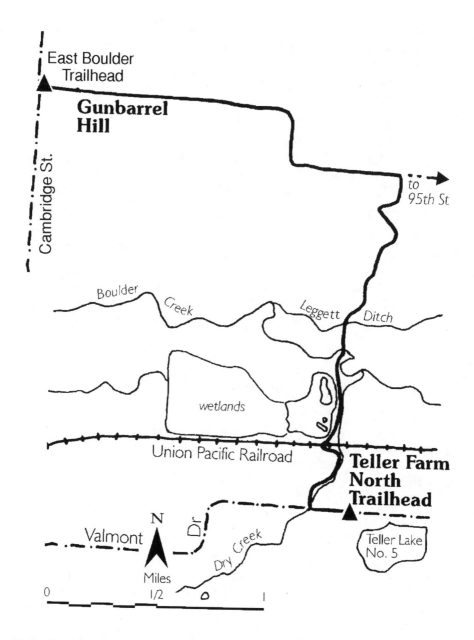

East Boulder Trail: White Rocks and Gunbarrel Farm Sections

Space Department. Farmer Howard Morton plowed the last sod in 1938 and remembers hitting buffalo wallows with his plow. After it became open space, the eroded land was reseeded and allowed to revert to native grasses such as sideoats grama, blue grama, and bluestem. Ring-necked pheasants are sometimes seen here.

Connections

At the southeast end of the Teller Farm North Trailhead parking lot on Valmont Road, you can pick up the **East Boulder Trail/Teller Lakes Section** (see page 18) or you can take the short, wheelchair-accessible trail to Teller Lake No. 5 to fish or watch the waterfowl. At the T-junction where the main trail heads to Gunbarrel Hill, a 0.5-mile segment leads to the White Rocks Trailhead on 95th Street.

Access

Park at the Teller Farm North Trailhead on Valmont Road, about 1 mile west of 95th Street. The trail can also be reached from the White Rocks Trailhead, about a mile north of the intersection of Valmont and 95th Street, or from the Gunbarrel Trailhead at Cambridge and Boulderado streets.

East Boulder Trail: Teller Lakes Section

Distance: 2.2 miles one way
Elevation: 5,200 feet with negligible elevation change
Highlights: Teller Lakes, fishing, waterbirds and raptors, mountain views, agricultural surroundings
Difficulty: Easy
Topo map: Niwot

Description

This level trail (actually old farm roads) winds through farmland, crosses a small irrigation ditch and the Leyner-Cottonwood #1 Irrigation Ditch, and connects Valmont and Arapahoe roads. Hawks frequently are seen soaring overhead or sitting in the cottonwoods that border the fields where crops are still raised. A short spur from the southern end of the trail leads to two of the Teller Lakes, where there is a fishing pier. These lakes and a small wetland provide habitats for many different waterbirds. This trail is on City of Boulder Open Space and is well marked.

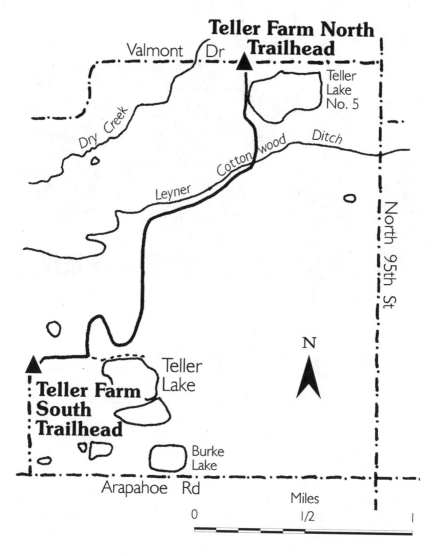

Teller Farm North Trailhead

Valmont Dr

Teller Lake No. 5

Dry Creek

Cottonwood Ditch

Leyner

North 95th St

N

Teller Lake

Teller Farm South Trailhead

Burke Lake

Arapahoe Rd

Miles

0   1/2   1

East Boulder Trail: Teller Lakes Section

View from Teller Lakes

History

The lakes are named for Senator Henry Teller, who served thirty years in the U.S. Senate and was appointed Secretary of the Interior in 1882. Senator Teller and William A. Davidson, whose name is attached to Davidson Mesa and to Davidson Ditch, owned much of the land in this area. Davidson Mesa is the hill on US 36 where the magical view of Boulder opens up below. Davidson Ditch is just west of the Mesa. The unpainted barn, built by Davidson around 1870, still stands just north of Valmont Road on the White Rocks section of East Boulder Trail.

Connections

At the Teller Farm North Trailhead, you can pick up the **East Boulder Trail/White Rocks and Gunbarrel Farm Section** (see page 16) at the northwest end of the parking lot or you can take the short, wheelchair-accessible trail to Teller Lake No. 5.

Access

Park either at the Teller Farm North Trailhead on Valmont Road, or at the Teller Farm South Trailhead on Arapahoe Road. Both areas are about 1 mile east of 75th Street.

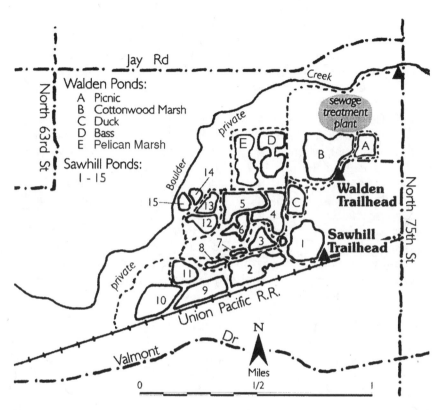

Walden and Sawhill Ponds

Walden and Sawhill Ponds

Distance: 1.2 miles from Cottonwood Marsh to west end of Sawhill
Elevation: About 5,100 feet with no elevation change
Highlights: Some of the best birding in Boulder, red foxes, white-tailed and mule deer, fishing, mountain views reflected in ponds
Difficulty: Easy
Topo map: Niwot

Description

This network of ponds, marshes, brush, and cottonwoods is more conducive to wandering and nature watching than to linear hiking and vigorous exercise. It's difficult to get lost while meandering along the old roads that are now closed to motorized vehicles. Sawhill Ponds (the southern section) is owned by the Colorado Division of Wildlife and managed by Boulder Open Space and Mountain Parks. Walden Ponds (the northern section) is operated by the County Parks and Open Space Department. But as far as hikers and wildlife are concerned, the area is one wondrous unit.

Our favorite route starts at the Cottonwood Marsh boardwalk (Walden section), where we look for shorebirds in the shallows. At the southwest end of the marsh, head toward the administration buildings, which serve as field offices for Boulder County Parks and Open Space. Cross the gravel road to Duck Pond and go through the opening in the fence into the Sawhill section. Walk west past several ponds to the cottonwood forest at the west end. You'll find lots of warblers here in the spring, and fireflies in early summer. Turn south and continue until you reach the large open pond north of the railroad track. Walk east toward the Sawhill entrance. Just before you reach the large pond west of the parking lot, turn north. At this point you can see the Walden section and can return to the Cottonwood Marsh boardwalk by walking north between several ponds.

Watch for red fox, deer, beaver, muskrat, and a great variety of shorebirds and waterbirds. In spring, great horned owls nest in the cottonwood forest and Canada geese nest on the islands.

History

The Sawhill Ponds were mined for gravel from 1958 to the early 1970s when the wetlands were largely restored. Some gravel mining still occurs along the periphery, but wildlife thrives. In fact, there are more deer here now than in 1900 when George Sawhill, a member of the family that owned the land for many years, was a boy. He could not recall seeing deer in the area when he was growing up. In 1998 gravel mining at Walden was completed, and "Pelican Marsh," the largest pond in the combined complex, was created.

Connections

The numerous old roads allow for a great variety of possible loops. You can also connect with the **Heatherwood-Walden Trail** at the 75th Street wastewater treatment plant north of Cottonwood Marsh and follow Boulder Creek to a parking area at 75th Street just south of Jay Road.

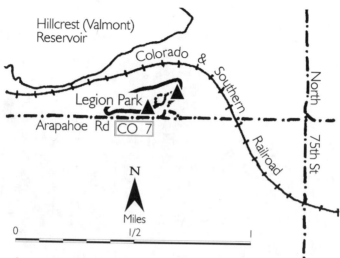

Cannon Loop Trail

Access

This area is west off of 75th Street, between Jay and Valmont Roads. For the Sawhill section, turn west onto the road just north of the railroad track. The Walden turnoff is also to the west, and is north of the Sawhill section. It is marked by a sign between the railroad track and the sewage treatment plant.

Cannon Loop Trail

Distance: 1 mile round-trip
Elevation: 5,360 feet with negligible elevation change
Highlights: Waterbirds on Valmont Reservoir, prairie dogs, mountain views, overview of Boulder
Difficulty: Easy
Topo map: Niwot

Description

This trail begins to the left of the cannon displayed at Legion Park (off of east Arapahoe Road) and circles below the perimeter of Goodview Hill,

The cannon on the Cannon Loop Trail

so called because it once served as a lookout for early Native Americans and white settlers. Excellent views of the Indian Peaks and of Valmont, Hillcrest, and Leggett-Owens Reservoirs can be seen from this trail. A large prairie dog town attracts bald eagles and other raptors. Many uncommon waterbirds, such as wood ducks, loons, and trumpeter swans have been seen on the reservoirs. An osprey nesting box was built in the spring of 2000 after the "fish eagles" had tried unsuccessfully to nest on the power towers for several years.

Because this trail is so short and easily accessible from Boulder, it's a good place for a lunch-hour walk and picnic.

History

In the late 1800s, Frank Weisenhorn built an icehouse here on what was then called "Owens Lake" to supply his Boulder City Brewing Company in Boulder. Townspeople came for picnicking, boating, ice skating, dancing, and an occasional balloon ride. A dance pavilion extended over the water at the southeast corner of the lake. Public Service Company began operating the electric plant here, with one stack, in 1918. The American Legion Post No. 10 landscaped the area in 1933 as a memorial to the soldiers of World War I and installed two World War I cannons on the hilltop.

Connections

There are no hiking connections to this trail, but the historic **Valmont Cemetery** is nearby and worth strolling through. From east Arapahoe Avenue, drive north on 63rd Street for 1 mile. Just before reaching Valmont Butte, turn east on a small dirt road that goes to the cemetery, now owned by Boulder Historic Society and dedicated to the memory of Boulder County Pioneers.

Access

Take Arapahoe Avenue east past the Valmont Power Plant and go 0.9 mile east of 63rd Street. Turn north onto a short gravel road at the Legion Park sign. Park at the turnaround on top of Goodview Hill.

Boulder Creek Path

Distance: 7 miles one way
Elevation: 5,800 feet at Fourmile Canyon to 5,200 feet at Valmont Lake
Highlights: People-, bird-, and fish-watching, tumultuous creek, catch-and-release fishing, gardens
Difficulty: Easy to moderate, depending on distance hiked
Topo map: Boulder, Niwot

Description

Stretching from east Boulder to the junction of Boulder and Fourmile Canyons, this trail along Boulder Creek cuts through the heart of the city, attracting crowds of hikers, joggers, skaters, and bicyclists. Because of the heavy use, most of the trail is paved. The section from Point o' Rocks (one mile west of Eben G. Fine Park) to 28th Street includes signs on the history and natural history of the area.

The trail is beautiful in all seasons: Naturalized bulbs bloom in early spring, waves of warblers arrive in May, large willows and cottonwoods provide summer shade and autumn color, and a luminario walk is sometimes held in winter. Special points of interest include a demonstration xeriscape garden (west of 6th Street), a children's fishing pond and a sculpture garden (west of 9th Street), the International Peace

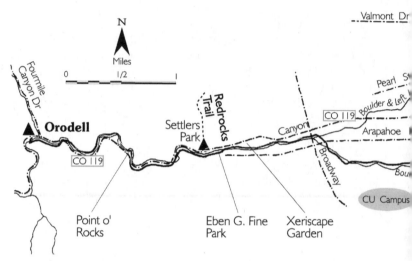

Boulder Creek Path

Garden (near Boulder Public Library), and a stream observatory (near Folsom Street).

To avoid collisions with bicyclists and rollerbladers, it's important to keep to the right and to be aware of other users. Unless you're feeling gregarious, the best time for this trail is early morning. You can start at any point and go for a few blocks or for the entire distance.

History

Although a tollroad had been built up Boulder Canyon to Magnolia Road in 1865, it was not extended to Nederland (then called Middle Boulder) until 1871, when silver was discovered at Caribou. In fact, according to Boulder historian Amos Bixby, "The settlers found Boulder Cañon so difficult of access that a man could not make his way up it by foot....It was a disputed question whether or not a wagon road could ever be constructed through it." Remnants of the tollroad and a retaining wall, built without mortar, can still be seen at Maxwell's Pitch (named for engineer James P. Maxwell, who was instrumental in building the road), just beyond the Point o' Rocks (also called the Elephant Buttresses). Maxwell also served as the

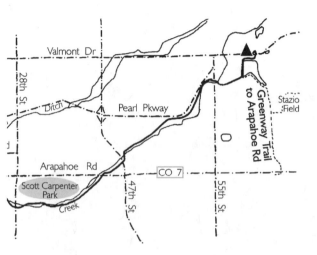

second mayor of Boulder and was a member of the territorial legislature and the first state senate.

During the late 1860s and 1870s, Martha Maxwell (James P. Maxwell's stepmother) and her husband James A. Maxwell lived in the area that is now Eben G. Fine Park, named for an early Boulder pharmacist and avid hiker. Martha became famous as one of the first female naturalists in the United States, and as a taxidermist who developed the idea of naturalistic dioramas in museums.

In 1883, the Greeley, Salt Lake, and Pacific narrow gauge railroad (called the Switzerland Trail) was completed to Sunset, a town about 4 miles west of Wall Street on CR 118, via Boulder and Fourmile Canyons. It was later extended to Ward and to Eldora. The railroad was washed out in 1894 during the worst flood in Boulder's history. Rebuilt in 1898, it was finally abandoned in 1919 when another flood wiped it out. Buttresses for this railroad can be seen near the Point o' Rocks.

In 1908, Frederick Law Olmsted Jr., noted landscape architect, was brought out from Harvard University to advise the city on future planning. In his *Improvement of Boulder County* report he wrote, "[K]eeping open for public use near the heart of the city a simple piece of pretty bottom-land of the very sort that Boulder Creek has been flooding over for countless centuries . . . would give a piece of recreation ground worth a great deal to

To Settlers Park from the Boulder Creek Path

the people. And at the same time it is probably the cheapest way of handling the flood problem of Boulder Creek."

Olmsted's advice was not heeded at the time and many municipal buildings, such as the jail and the public library, were built on the creek's banks. However, in the early 1970s city planners became concerned about the danger of flash flooding; therefore, additional buildings in the flood plain were prohibited.

The west end of the Boulder Creek Path terminates at the junction of Boulder and Fourmile Canyons, the former site of Orodell, a mining town that thrived during the 1870s. Much of the town burned in 1891, and the sawmill and gold mill were destroyed by the 1894 flood. Remains of a log structure here in Boulder Creek may be part of the dam for the original sawmill. The Orodell townsite (a Boulder County Historic Landmark) is now buried under some twenty feet of rubble deposited when SR 119 was improved and paved in 1953.

The first wheat in Colorado Territory was planted in 1860 by the Wellman Brothers (Henry, Luther, and Sylvanus) in forty acres bordering on Boulder Creek. Their field was at the present junction of 47th Street and Arapahoe Avenue on the north side of Arapahoe, a place where prairie dogs and cattle graze today.

Connections

At the west end of Eben G. Fine Park you can walk under Canyon Boulevard to Settlers Park and catch the trail up to **Red Rocks and Anemone Hill** (see page 70). Just beyond 17th Street, a bridge crosses Boulder Creek and a path leads up the hill to the **University of Colorado Campus,** an attractive place to stroll—especially in autumn. Several intersecting streets (6th, 9th, Broadway, and 13th) give access to the **Mapleton Historic District** and to the **Downtown Mall.** East of 55th Street, the trail veers away from Boulder Creek and goes south, paralleling South Boulder Creek. This section connects with **Centennial Trail** (see page 31) and **South Boulder Creek Trail** (see page 30).

Access

Eben G. Fine Park, at the mouth of Boulder Canyon on west Arapahoe Avenue, is the best access for the west end. Scott Carpenter Park, at 30th Street and Arapahoe Avenue, is a good access point for the middle section. A sidewalk west of the Stazio ballfields, west of 63rd Street between Valmont Road and Arapahoe Avenue, gives access to the eastern section. You can, however, pick up the trail at any point along Boulder Creek.

South Boulder Creek Trail

Distance: 3.5 miles one way
Elevation: 5,300 feet with little elevation change
Highlights: Tallgrass prairie, streamside habitat, tall cottonwoods and willows, white-tailed and mule deer
Difficulty: Easy
Topo map: Louisville

South Boulder Creek Trail

Description

This trail follows South Boulder Creek through riparian corridors and wetland meadows. Part of the trail goes through the Tallgrass Prairie Natural Area, where many species of native tallgrasses and wildflowers flourish, including a rare bog orchid, *Spiranthes diluvialis*. Such uncommon birds as rails, bobolinks, and great crested flycatchers are sometimes seen.

From the trailhead, go south. At 1.3 miles walk through the South Boulder Road Underpass, at which point the trail becomes a gravel service road heading west for 0.3 mile, paralleling South Boulder Road. At the access gate, turn south and continue for about 1.9 miles to Marshall Road. Wetlands and lakes near Marshall Road provide good waterfowl viewing.

Because of erosion caused by overuse near the trailhead, take care to stay on the trail.

History

The remains of the old Dorn Farm site are visible west of the trail just south of South Boulder Road, and the site of the Abernathy Dairy is visible east of the creek where the trail dead-ends.

Connections

From the Bobolink Trailhead, take the underpass beneath Baseline Road to link with the **Centennial Trail** (see next trail description). If you turn off from Centennial onto Old Tale Road, you can link with the Greenways Trail and the **Boulder Creek Path** (see page 25).

Access

Park at the Bobolink Trailhead, 0.1 mile west of the intersection of Baseline and Cherryvale Roads. There are connecting spurs (with parking) for East Boulder Community Center and for the historic Van Vleet Ranch on Cherryvale Road.

Centennial Trail

Distance: 1 mile one way
Elevation: 5,250 feet with negligible elevation gain
Highlights: Streamside habitat, llama farm
Difficulty: Easy
Topo map: Niwot

Description

This paved trail connects Dimmit Drive and 55th Street. From Dimmit Drive it follows South Boulder Creek to a junction with Empson irrigation ditch, at which point it turns west. It skirts a llama farm and the Flatirons Municipal Golf Course, where Canada geese patrol the grounds. Willows shade most of the trail and provide habitat for warblers and other songbirds attracted to water. From 55th Street, you can continue west a short way along Empson Ditch through residential neighborhoods.

History

This trail was built in 1976 and dedicated as a local contribution to the United States bicentennial.

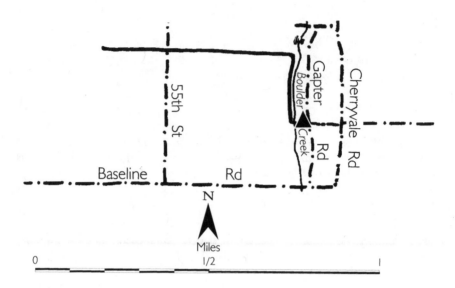

Centennial Trail

Connections

From Dimmit Drive, turn right (south) on Gapter Road and walk about 1 block to Baseline Road. Take the underpass to the **South Boulder Creek Trail** (see page 30). You can also connect with the **Boulder Creek Path** (see page 25) by following the signs north along Gaptor, McSorley, and Old Tale Roads.

Access

There is limited parking along 55th Street halfway between Arapahoe Avenue and Baseline Road at the Centennial Trailhead.There is better parking at the Bobolink Trailhead on Baseline Road.

Dry Creek Trail

Distance: 1-mile loop
Elevation: 5,300 feet with negligible elevation change
Highlights: Views across Baseline Reservoir to snowcapped mountains, waterbirds, agricultural surroundings, prairie dogs

Dry Creek Trail

Difficulty: Easy
Topo map: Louisville

Description

Follow the packed gravel trail past the prairie dog colony to the bridge across Dry Creek (a misnomer—it's not dry). Just west of the bridge, take either branch of the loop. The left branch follows Dry Creek, and the right branch heads west, eventually paralleling the shore of Baseline Reservoir. Although the reservoir is private, you can enjoy the spectacular view across the lake to the mountains. Bring a pair of binoculars to watch the waterbirds that frequent the lake and the raptors that prey on the prairie dogs. Along the southernmost segment of trail, look to the southeast for a glimpse of the old Walburga Abbey. The Dry Creek area,

Walburga Abbey from Dry Creek Trail

sometimes called "puppy park," is a favorite for walking and training dogs, so be aware that there will be numerous "poop baggies" along the trail as well as dogs.

Access

Park at the Dry Creek Trailhead south of Baseline Road and east of the Baseline Reservoir, about a mile east of Cherryvale Road.

CAROLYN HOLMBERG PRESERVE/ ROCK CREEK FARM

This working farm was purchased by Boulder County Open Space for agricultural preservation in 1980. Most of the 1,151 acres are leased, but several trails loop through the farm and past croplands. The main trailhead is at Stearns Lake, which is stocked with tiger muskie and channel catfish and is a good place to view shorebirds, ducks, and geese. The northwest side of the lake is a wildlife habitat, off-limits to public use. An old trailhead on Dillon Road also has been closed because burrowing owls, absent from the county for several years, returned to nest here in 2001.

Cradleboard Trail

Distance: 1.5 miles one way
Elevation: 5,282 feet with negligible elevation change
Highlights: Stearns Lake, birdwatching, fishing, prairie dogs, panoramic views
Difficulty: Easy
Topo map: Lafayette

Description

From Stearns Lake Trailhead, take the **Mary Miller Trail** around the south side of the lake. At the 0.25-mile point, the trail forks at a signpost with the left fork following the Mary Miller Trail to US 287. The Cradleboard Trail turns right and continues south across the bridge over Rock Creek.

In a short distance the trail heads west and eventually meets an extension of 104th Street. A right turn takes you to the Stearns Lake Trailhead. The main trail turns left and continues past a small pond to another junction. If you continue south at this point and cross the Burlington Northern railroad tracks, you will come to various Broomfield Open Space trails, including one to Josh's Pond. Cradleboard Trail heads west along Buffalo Gulch past a prairie dog town and a small wetland. Panoramic views of the Indian Peaks are highlights. This trail segment dead-ends at Brainard Road, so you should retrace your route to 104th Street, which leads back to Stearns Lake.

History

A recent archaeological dig in this vicinity uncovered numerous Native American artifacts as well as at least twenty-five fire pits, one of which is estimated to be 6,000 years old. The trail name pays homage to the Cheyenne and Arapaho women who formerly lived in the area and created extravagantly ornamented cradleboards.

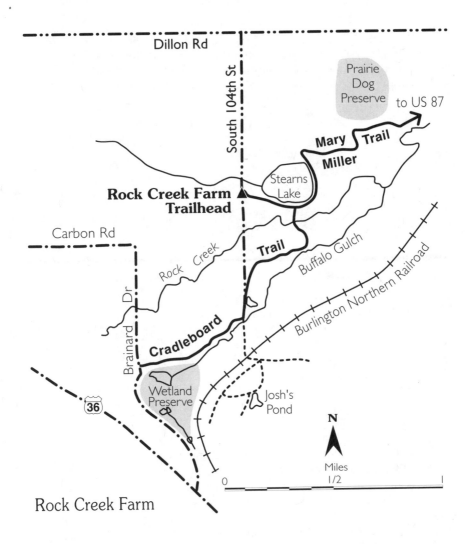

Rock Creek Farm

The farm dates back to 1864 when Lafayette and Mary Miller ran a stagecoach station and a roadhouse here as well as a farm, a cattle ranch, and an apple orchard. Their grandson recalled how Mary baked 100 apple pies one day and sold them for a dollar each when the circus camped nearby. Mary founded the town of Lafayette in 1888, naming it for her husband who died from heat stroke in 1878. Many of the buildings date from 1933 when W. S. Stearns operated a dairy farm here.

The name "Carolyn Holmberg Preserve" was added to Rock Creek Farm in 2000 to honor Carolyn Holmberg, director of Boulder County Parks and Open Space from 1983 until her death in 1998. She was instrumental in preserving 40,000 acres in the county, including Rock Creek Farm.

Connections

At the 0.25-mile point from the Stearns Lake Trailhead, the **Mary Miller Trail** diverges from Cradleboard and continues east 1.25 miles to US 287. The southward extension of Cradleboard forks several times, with one branch leading to **Josh's Pond** and another to Broomfield's **Lac Amora Open Space**. This network of trails is a work in progress. The master plan calls for eventually connecting the Mary Miller Trail to the Coal Creek Trail and possibly extending Cradleboard Trail westward.

Access

The farm is located northwest of Broomfield at the intersection of Dillon Road and South 104th Street. Stearns Lake Trailhead is on 104th Street a short distance south of Dillon Road.

Coal Creek Trail

Distance: 7 miles one way
Elevation: 5,278 feet with negligible elevation change
Highlights: Streamside habitat, birdwatching, prairie dogs
Difficulty: Easy
Topo map: Lafayette

Description

This urban trail traverses parts of Louisville and Lafayette, extending from 120th Street to Dillon Road with an underpass at US 287. It more or less parallels Coal Creek and passes through open space and residential and commercial areas. From the Aquarius Trailhead (roughly midway along the trail), you can either head west along a well-marked route toward Dillon Road or east toward 120th Street. Our favorite segment meanders to the east. This part of the trail follows the creek through a somewhat wilder habitat than the western segment and is shaded by numerous cottonwoods. Despite noisy planes from the nearby airport, wildlife is relatively plentiful along the creek corridor. Look for herons, snipe, woodpeckers, and bank

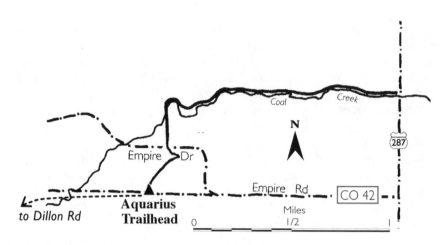

Coal Creek Trail

swallows in the summer and for lacy hoarfrost early on a winter morning. From the US 287 underpass, you can continue on to US 120 or take the paved bike path to Baseline Road. Note that work is still being done on some segments of the trail.

History

Louisville and Lafayette grew up around the coal industry and were largely settled by coal miners. Louis Nawatny established Louisville in 1878 shortly after he discovered the first coal in the area. The town is named for him.

Coal was discovered in the Lafayette area in 1887. The following year Mary Miller, widow of Lafayette Miller, founded the town, naming it for her husband. Later she helped open the town's first school, and legend has it that she once read a set of encyclopedias cover to cover. Mary Miller also opened Lafayette's first bank, becoming the first female bank president in the world. See page 36 for additional information on the Millers.

Connections

The trail is slated to connect eventually with **Rock Creek Farm** (see page 34), Broomfield's **Lac Amora** open space, and Superior.

Access

Park at Aquarius Trailhead on SR 42 (also called Empire Road) 1.3 miles west of US 287.

Hikers amidst rime frost along Coal Creek Trail

5/7/03

Marshall Mesa, Community Ditch, Greenbelt Plateau

Distance: 2.4 miles one way
Elevation: 5,550 to 5,900 feet
Highlights: Coal mining ruins, irrigation ditches, mountain views, grasslands, wildflowers, raptors
Difficulty: Easy
Topo map: Louisville

Description

You can hike this trail conveniently from either direction and make several loops and interesting detours. Starting at the Marshall Mesa Trailhead, follow the trail for 0.8 mile up to Community Ditch (built in 1885), crossing another, lower irrigation ditch along the way. (If you hike east along this lower ditch, you will find coal mine ruins.) On top of Marshall Mesa, great horned owls frequently nest in the ponderosa pines, and sandstone formations provide habitat for early wildflowers.

When you reach Community Ditch, turn west and follow the ditch to the junction for Greenbelt Plateau. Cross the bridge and climb gently to the plateau and the wide-open spaces of the prairie, continuing on to the Greenbelt Plateau Trailhead. The Greenbelt Plateau Trail was once part of the main route from Boulder to Golden. You can leave a car here if you want to do a one-way hike, or you can return to the Marshall Mesa Trailhead, making some of the detours suggested on page 42.

History

In the 1860s, shortly after coal was discovered in this area, Joseph M. Marshall built the first blast furnace to manufacture pig iron and purchased several of the existing mines. At various times, the coal mining town was called Foxtown, Langford, Gorham, and, finally, Marshall. It contained eight hundred residents and three saloons—a larger metropolis than Boulder at the time. Even then, people were concerned about air pollution and complained about the smoke from a twelve-ton steam engine used to haul the coal to market. Numerous underground coal fires have flared since those early days of mining, and some are still burning. The fires may have been started by poor mining practices, by strikers, or by moonshine stills hidden in the mines; no one knows for sure.

During the coal wars from 1910 to 1914, soldiers with machine guns were sometimes posted on the south slopes of the mesa. No miners were

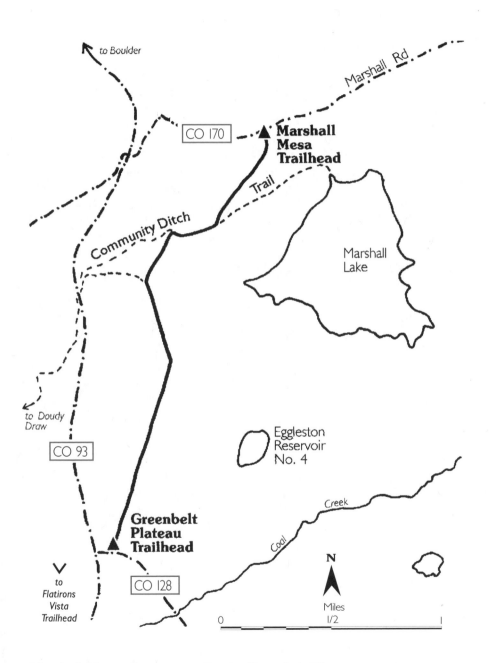

Marshall Mesa, Community Ditch, Greenbelt Plateau

shot at Marshall, but six were killed by the National Guard at the Columbine Mine in Erie in 1927.

On-site displays and brochures are being prepared by the Boulder City Open Space Department on the history of the Marshall area.

Connections

If you turn east at the point where the Marshall Mesa section joins Community Ditch, you will reach an overlook of privately owned **Marshall Lake** in 0.8 mile. If you continue west on Community Ditch past the Greenbelt Plateau cutoff, you reach SR 93, at which point you can cross the highway and continue along Community Ditch to **Doudy Draw** (see page 110). You can also stay on the east side of the highway, cross Community Ditch, and rejoin the Greenbelt Plateau Trail in 0.3 mile. At the Greenbelt Plateau Trailhead, you can continue to the **Flatirons Vista Trailhead** and continue west to **Doudy Draw.**

Access

Park at the Marshall Mesa Trailhead on the south side of Marshall Road, 0.9 mile east of SR 93, or at the Greenbelt Plateau Trailhead, 0.1 mile east of SR 93 on the north side of SR 128.

Foothills

Boulder County has preserved some of the foothills area at elevations from approximately 5,500 to 8,000 feet, where a number of excellent trail systems exist. Though many of the trails described here are very steep, they offer a fascinating link between plains and peaks and frequently culminate in views of Boulder Valley to the east and snowcapped mountains to the west. The ecosystems extend from shrublands to ponderosa pine and Douglas-fir forests, supporting a wide variety of birds, mammals, and other wildlife.

We prefer to hike these trails, which range from easy to strenuous, in spring and fall when temperatures are moderate, but they are also pleasant early or late in the day in summer. In winter, the more level trails, such as the Mesa Trail, are good for ski touring after a heavy snowfall, but as the snow melts skiers should beware of rocks and hikers should look out for icy spots.

Button Rock Preserve Loop

Distance: 6-mile loop
Elevation: 5,960 to 6,420 feet
Highlights: Ralph Price Reservoir, wildlife, wildflowers, red and buff sandstone formations, cascading creek, waterfalls, fishing (limited permits available)
Difficulty: Moderate
Topo map: Lyons

Description

Walking west along the gravel road (CR 80, closed to traffic except for authorized vehicles), you pass the wide waterfall pouring over Longmont Reservoir Dam. A short distance beyond the long, narrow reservoir, and just before the road crosses to the right-hand side of the North St. Vrain Creek, there is a large sign for the Sleepy Lion Trail on the left. Take the Sleepy Lion Trail, which heads uphill to the left of the gravel road. This trail climbs through ponderosa pine and Douglas-fir forest and an open meadow. Just before it descends to the foot of the Button Rock Dam,

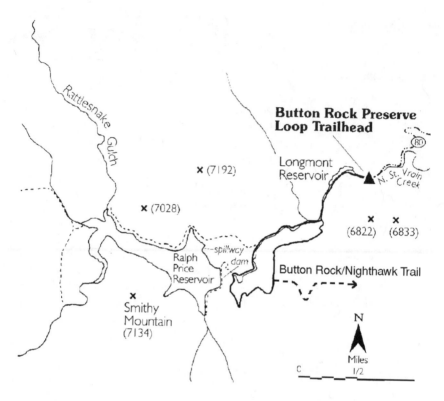

Button Rock Preserve Loop

the trail passes through an area of red rock formations and drops into a small canyon.

At the foot of Button Rock Dam, the North St. Vrain Creek shoots out forcefully from a small opening. To reach the top of the dam and the shore of Ralph Price Reservoir, take the trail that zigzags up the right-hand side of the dam.

Although no trails circle the reservoir, a trail continues for about half a mile on the left-hand side. Another 3-mile trail on the right-hand side goes to the inlet on the northwest end of the reservoir. If water is flowing over the spillway and blocking the north shore, you can head down the gravel road a short distance and follow the signs back up (about one quarter-mile) to the ranger cottage, detouring around the spillway. (Note: mileage is

Ralph Price Reservoir

given for the loop up to the reservoir and back and does not include these shoreline trails, which may be extended in the future.)

Returning to the parking area via the road is easier and shorter than the trail because there is no elevation gain. Brown and rainbow trout abound in North St. Vrain Creek, which parallels the road, as well as in the reservoirs. However, fishing permits are limited. The surrounding area is a wildlife preserve open to walk-in visitors only. Look for dippers, pygmy owls, and golden eagles. In winter, bald eagles roost around the reservoir, and in summer swallows nest along the cliffs. Bighorn sheep can be seen in some of the more remote areas.

History

Below North and South Sheep Mountains, north of Ralph Price Reservoir, are the fast-disappearing remains of the Sheep Mountain Ranch, an old homestead that was later used by naturalists to study bighorn sheep. This area was a traditional lambing ground for bighorns, which were reintroduced into the area in 1980. Rocky Mountain National Park naturalists are studying the sheep to determine migration corridors between their summering and wintering grounds.

The City of Longmont built Ralph Price Reservoir, named for a former mayor of Longmont, between 1967–1969. The Sleepy Lion Trail
is named for a mountain lion who once grabbed a forty-five-minute cat-
nap there.

Connections

From the northwest end of Ralph Price Reservoir, old roads connect to
the **Coulson Gulch Trail** (FS Trail 916) in Higgins Park. The downhill
branch of Coulson Gulch drops to North St. Vrain Creek, and the uphill
branch climbs to Johnny Park. It's possible to leave one car at the Coulson
Gulch Trailhead (4.5 miles from US 36 via the Big Elk Meadows turnoff)
and another at the Button Rock barricade for a one-way hike of about 6.5
miles. However, the trail is indistinct on the south side of Rattlesnake Gulch
and some rock scrambling is required. The Boulder County topo map is essential if you try this route.

Just before Sleepy Lion Trail drops down to the reservoir, Button Rock
Trail (completed in 1999) links to Nighthawk Trail and Hall Ranch. You can
do a 16-mile one-way hike by leaving cars at both Hall Ranch and Button
Rock Trailheads.

Access

Take US 36 north from Boulder to Lyons. From Lyons, drive 4 miles
on US 36 toward Estes Park, turn left on CR 80, continue for 3 miles to
the Button Rock barricade, and park along the road.

Rabbit Mountain: Little Thompson Overlook Trail

Distance: 1.5 miles one way
Elevation: 5,500 to 6,000 feet
Highlights: Views from prairie to peaks, raptors, prairie dogs, tepee rings
Difficulty: Easy to moderate
Topo map: Carter Lake, Hygiene

Description

From the picnic pavilion walk uphill below a colorful escarpment to a
low saddle with panoramic views of the plains. At the signpost turn left and
follow the trail through stands of mountain mahogany, yucca, native

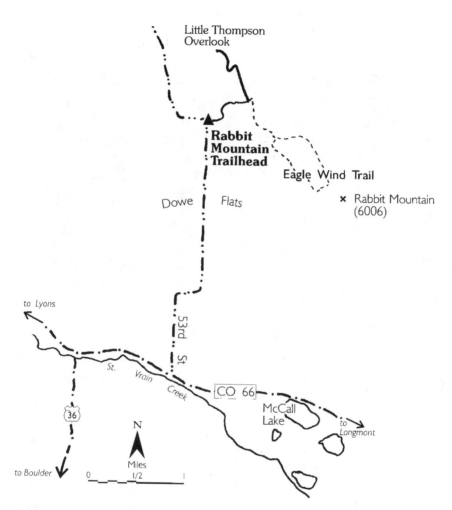

Rabbit Mountain: Little Thompson Overlook Trail

grasses, and wildflowers to an overlook at the top of the ridge. The overlook is on private property so access is not guaranteed.

This area was once called Rattlesnake Mountain—for good reasons.
Watch for rattlers and also for the beautiful bull snakes, which we see more
frequently than the similar appearing rattlers. From the overlook you can
see down into the multicolored rock formations of Little Thompson
Canyon. Longs Peak, Mount Meeker, and the Indian Peaks are to the west.

View from overlook of Little Thompson Canyon. Carter Lake is in background.

From some points along the trail you can see Pikes Peak to the south on a clear day. Look for bald eagles (in winter), golden eagles, other raptors, and coyotes attracted by the prairie dogs. Also look for deer and for evidence of faulting and earthquakes.

Return to parking area via this same route. In the future, a connecting trail may be built to Carter Lake in Larimer County.

History

Native Americans lived and hunted here for at least five thousand years. The Arapaho used the area most recently, and tepee rings (large circles outlined by partially buried stones) show where they once camped. A large prairie dog colony now inhabits the main encampment. Any artifacts you happen upon, including tepee ring stones, should be left in place.

The first white settler, Columbus Weese, arrived in 1864 and started farming. His daughter married Jack Moomaw, the first National Park Service Ranger on the east side of the Continental Divide. Because Moomaw strongly favored wilderness preservation, his granddaughter sold the land to the Boulder County Parks and Open Space Department in 1984.

Connections

At the signpost on the saddle, turn right and cross a gravel road to another signpost. **Indian Mesa Trail** follows the road a short distance, turns right at the next signpost, and crosses the mesa to dead-end in 1.6 miles. **Eagle Wind Trail** follows the ridge south to make an approximately 3-mile loop. The summit of Rabbit Mountain is closed seasonally to protect golden eagle nesting habitat. Please respect all closures posted in the area.

Access

Turn north onto 53rd Street from the Ute Highway (SR 66) between the towns of Lyons and Longmont. Continue about 2 miles to the Rabbit Mountain Trailhead.

HALL RANCH

Bitterbrush Trail and Nelson Loop

Distance: 9.3 miles round-trip
Elevation: 5,440 to 6,820 feet
Highlights: Pink- and salmon-colored sandstone formations; mountain and canyon views; historic ranch ruins; prairie dogs, raptors, and other wildlife; wildflowers
Difficulty: Moderate to strenuous
Topo map: Lyons

Description

The Bitterbrush Trail starts on a south-facing slope dominated by mountain mahogany and three-leaf sumac. Look north for stunning views of Hat Rock and Indian Lookout Mountain whose orange-pink rock is especially dramatic in late afternoon. The trail is named for the bitterbrush, also called antelope brush, that flourishes along the trail—a sign that the area has not been overgrazed. Because this shrub is relished by both wildlife and livestock, botanists use it to evaluate range condition.

The trail ascends through juniper and ponderosa pines to a ridgetop overlooking one of the highest prairie dog colonies in the county at 6,200 feet. At 3.5 miles the Bitterbrush Trail joins the 2.3-mile Nelson Ranch Loop where a short spur leads to the Nelson ranch house and a cement silo

Hall Ranch

in Antelope Park. Dramatic views of Longs Peak and Mt. Meeker and of the pink palisades above the North St. Vrain Valley appear to the west and north. You can return by either the same route or the Nighthawk Trail (see the "Connections" section).

Wildlife abounds in the varied habitats of Hall Ranch. Both Hall and Heil Ranches are important elk migration corridors, one of the few places where elk can freely migrate from mountains to plains. Also watch for mountain lions, bobcats, badgers, bighorns, wild turkeys, and prairie rattlers. Wildflowers range from lavender pasqueflowers and yellow violets in spring to lavender asters and yellow sunflowers in fall. We especially delight in the pink-flowering ball cactus found at the higher elevations in late April and May.

This trail is very popular with both hikers and mountain bikers even on weekdays. To avoid crowds, go early in the morning, or try the Nighthawk Trail where bicyclists are prohibited. Dogs are not permitted on Hall Ranch.

History

This 3,205-acre ranch was earlier inhabited by Arapaho and Cheyenne Indians who hunted bison, deer, and elk here. In 1890, Richard Clark homesteaded the land, later selling it to the Nelson family, who built a wooden home and a concrete silo in Antelope Park. Over the years more than twenty families have lived and farmed on what is now Hall Ranch, but most of their homes are in ruins. Hallwyn and June Hall bought the ranch

Bitterbrush and Nelson Loop at Hall Ranch

in 1944. Their stone house (built in 1890) and other outbuildings near the highway are currently closed to the public. Because John Hall and his family wanted the land preserved, they sold it to Boulder County Open Space in 1993. Many buildings on Boulder's University of Colorado campus are built from stone quarried in the area.

Connections

The 4.1-mile **Nighthawk Trail** begins at the Bitterbrush Trailhead and joins the Nelson Loop at the far southwest corner. You can return via the same route or via the Bitterbrush Trail. **Button Rock Trail**, a link to **Sleepy Lion Trail**, also connects to the Nighthawk Trail near the upper end. If you leave one car at the Button Rock parking area and another at Hall Ranch, you can enjoy an 8-mile trek from the North St. Vrain area to the South St. Vrain.

Access

From Lyons go west on SR 7 for 1.7 miles to the turnoff for the parking lot on the right side of the road.

HEIL RANCH

Lichen Loop, Wapiti Trail, Ponderosa Loop

Distance: 1.3 miles round-trip (Lichen Loop), 2.5 miles one way (Wapiti Trail), 5.2 miles round-trip (Ponderosa Loop)
Elevation: 5,900 to 6,680 feet
Highlights: Wildlife; wildflowers; birdwatching; interesting geology and rock formations; historic ruins; views of mountains, canyons, and plains
Difficulty: Easy to moderate
Topo map: Lyons

Description

Because of the diverse ecosystems, wildlife abounds at Heil Ranch, one of the most important elk migration corridors in the county. Mountain lions, bobcats, black bears, mule deer, globally rare butterflies, wild turkeys, and raptors also thrive. We once spotted two golden eagles, one of them carrying a prairie dog. Several old roads throughout the ranch are closed to public use and dogs are prohibited to protect the wildlife and to preserve the habitat.

Various hiking permutations can be made by combining Lichen and Ponderosa Loops and the connecting Wapiti Trail. Lichen Loop crosses an intermittent stream called Plumely Creek at Kiosk Bridge near the upper parking area and heads gently uphill. Soon after the trail forks, the right branch crosses over unusual examples of stromatolites, reddish rocks formed by lime-secreting blue-green algae. These formations, sometimes called "fossilized algae," are usually found in marine environments. Look for ice cream scoop–size rocks with concentric rings. At the fork, take either branch and head up through meadows of native grasses and shrubs and past colorful lichen-covered boulders. In the ponderosa and Douglas fir forest at the far end of the loop, a connecting trail to Wapiti branches to the right.

Wapiti Trail starts at the upper parking lot and follows an old farm road along Plumely Creek. The trail soon departs from the creek and heads uphill past a prairie dog colony and into a ponderosa pine forest where jays, woodpeckers, and nuthatches flourish and where spring beauties proliferate in April.

Ponderosa Loop, which starts 2.5 miles up from the trailhead, balloons off of the Wapiti Trail. We like to take the right branch first. Along the way you pass the stone foundations for several temporary cabins built to satisfy

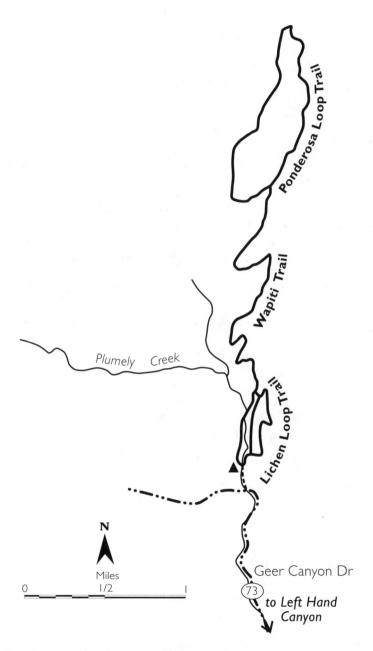

Ponderosa Loop Trail

Wapiti Trail

Plumely Creek

Lichen Loop Trail

N

Miles
0   1/2   1

Geer Canyon Dr

73 *to Left Hand Canyon*

Lichen Loop, Wapiti Trail, Ponderosa Loop

homesteading requirements, the remains of a substantial stone house, and several old quarries. Eventually, views of the South St. Vrain Canyon, **Hall Ranch,** and orange-pink rock formations such as Hat Rock and Indian Lookout Mountain open up below. At the high point, an overlook offers spectacular views of Longs, Meeker, and Sawtooth peaks. Continue on the trail to close the loop.

History

Four prehistoric Native American sites testify to the early use of this area, dating back 5,000 years. Later, Arapaho and Cheyenne Indians hunted and gathered in the valley, which was first homesteaded in 1888 by Solomon Geer. Geer's arm was mutilated in a farm accident and had to be amputated without anesthetics, but he continued ranching into his seventies. Several other families later homesteaded in the area. In 1996, Boulder County Open Space purchased 4,923 acres from the Heil family, who still ranch the area south of the trailhead.

Access

From US 36 north of Boulder, turn onto Lefthand Canyon Road. Go 0.6 mile and turn onto Geer Canyon Drive. Continue 1.25 miles to the parking area and trailhead.

Bald Mountain Scenic Area: "Pines-to-Peak" Trail

Distance: 1.5-mile loop
Elevation: 6,921 to 7,161 feet
Highlights: Views of peaks and plains, ponderosa pine habitat, deer
Difficulty: Easy
Topo map: Boulder

Description

Starting at the Bald Mountain picnic area, the "Pines-to-Peak" Trail goes through meadows and ponderosa pines to Bald Mountain (7,161 feet) and loops back to the picnic area. Along the well-marked trail are vistas of the plains and the foothills to the east and of the Continental Divide to the west. Because of its intermediate elevation, this area is good for off-season hikes. It is also a good place to take out-of-state visitors who are not yet acclimated.

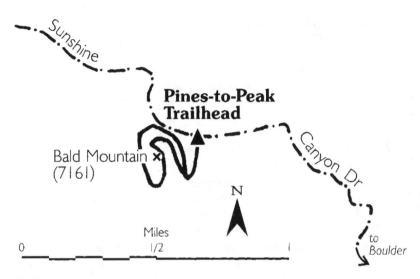

Bald Mountain Scenic Area: "Pines-to-Peak" Trail

History

An old corral and chute near the park entrance are historical remains of an 1886 homestead where cattle were raised. Ten years later, Frank and John Weist commenced mining in the area. Some of their exploratory pits can still be seen in the Bald Mountain Scenic Area, which, in 1973, became the first park opened by the Boulder County Parks and Open Space Department.

The road up Sunshine Canyon was originally a military road called the Gordon-McHenry Road. It was named for the engineers who built it in the early 1860s and possibly was used by the army to intercept and attack Mormons on their way to Deseret. Intended to cross Arapaho Pass, the Gordon-McHenry Road turned west at Poorman Road and eventually petered out on the flats north of Caribou. Remnants of it can still be seen above Fourmile Canyon.

Access

The trailhead and picnic areas are 5 miles west of Boulder on the south side of Sunshine Canyon Drive. Sunshine Canyon is a continuation of Mapleton Avenue west of 4th Street.

Sugarloaf Mountain

Distance: 0.5 mile one way
Elevation: 8,340 to 8,917 feet
Highlights: Spectacular views of peaks and plains
Difficulty: Easy
Topo map: Gold Hill

Description

Sugarloaf is the symmetrical, conical mountain that dominates the foothills above Boulder. The trail provides a quick, somewhat steep workout with a reward at the top—views that encompass the Mummy Range, Longs Peak, the Indian Peaks, and Mount Evans. Below, the plains seem to stretch to infinity, and the many reservoirs sparkle like blue topazes. For sheer magic, pick a clear night when snow covers the peaks to the west, and time your hike to arrive at the summit at sunrise to see alpenglow on the mountains.

No signs mark the route, but it's easy to find. From the parking area, cross the road to the east. Go past a gate and head up the old (and stony) mining road, now closed to motorized vehicles. Douglas fir, ponderosa pine, stunted aspen groves, and lots of kinnikinnick line the road. As you near the exposed top, vegetation gives way to sandstone slabs of talus and blackened tree snags, a result of the 1989 Black Tiger wildfire. The site of this raging fire that nearly destroyed the hillside community is now peaceful and teems with many species of wildflowers. Listen for nuthatches and woodpeckers.

History

In July 1989 the temperature hit 100 degrees for two days in a row. On July 9 the horrendous Black Tiger fire started, eventually burning 2,000 acres. The fire started in Black Tiger Gulch, named for a Ute woman who taught a local doctor, Maggie Livingston, many of her herbal cures.

Sugarloaf was a favorite hiking trail in the 1960s. Later, the privately owned trail was closed to the public, and an out-of-state landowner planned to build a trophy home at the very top. Fortunately, in 1995 the Boulder County Open Space Department stepped in and purchased the summit.

Connections

At the parking area, Sugarloaf Mountain Road joins the Switzerland Trail, an old narrow-gauge railroad bed that connected Ward to Eldora and to Boulder. One of our favorite autumn hikes is along the spur of the Switzerland Trail that heads west toward Glacier Lake from the parking

View from Sugarloaf's summit

area. There is little traffic on this stretch, and the aspen and asters are superb in late September.

Access

About a mile west of the tunnel in Boulder Canyon (SR 119), turn right onto Sugarloaf Road. Head uphill 4.9 miles to a dirt road called Sugarloaf Mountain Road. Turn right and continue another 0.8 mile to the unmarked parking area.

Anne U. White Trail

Distance: 1.5 miles one way
Elevation: 6,040 to 6,600 feet
Highlights: Lush streamside habitat, small waterfalls and pools, wildflowers, mossy rocks
Difficulty: Easy
Topo map: Boulder

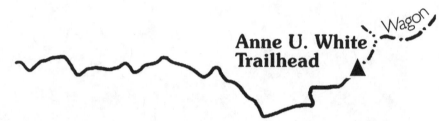

Anne U. White Trailhead

Anne U. White Trail

Description

The trail goes gently uphill along Fourmile Canyon Creek, crossing it twenty-two times before dead-ending at private property. The stream is small, so crossings are no problem. Along the way, you pass many little pools, miniature waterfalls, and groves of aspen. Higher on the ridge, ponderosa pines and Douglas-fir predominate. Spring wildflowers such as shooting stars, sugarbowls, penstemon, and pasqueflowers are prolific, and the running water attracts a variety of birds. Mountain lions and nesting hummingbirds have been seen here.

Less than one mile up the trail atop a small hill, a sandstone bench invites hikers to sit and watch for wildlife along the stream below or on the rock formations across the canyon. Farther up, the trail passes through a small meadow and divides with the left fork following the stream and the right fork climbing slightly higher. The two branches rejoin shortly before reaching a round pool fed by a small waterfall. The area is pungent with spearmint. Beyond this point, the canyon opens up a bit and the trail dead-ends below a rock outcropping.

This trail may eventually be extended to the **Bald Mountain Scenic Area** and the **Betasso area** (see pages 54 and 65).

History

The trail is named in memory of Anne Underwood White (1919–1989), who was a geographer, writer, and local advocate of many worth-

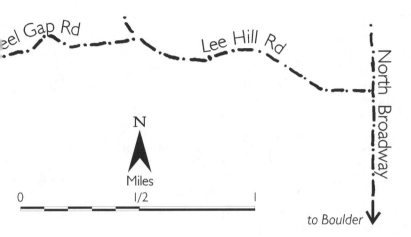

while causes, including open space. Anne U. White was a member of the Boulder Parks and Open Space Advisory Committee and championed the concept of trail corridors. She and her husband, Gilbert White, donated twenty acres as part of this trail. In 1983 she wrote, "This steep little canyon is one of the few canyons near Boulder which has not yet had a road driven through it. It is a green and pleasant place with its rocky cliffs and ephemeral winding stream."

Access

From North Broadway, turn west onto Lee Hill Road and drive 1.1 miles to Wagonwheel Gap Road. Turn left and go 1 mile. Turn left again onto a dirt road that dead-ends in 0.2 mile. Park alongside the road.

Forsythe Canyon Creek

Distance: 1 mile one way
Elevation: 7,760 to 7,400 feet
Highlights: Waterfall, lush streamside habitat, wildflowers, secluded inlet of Gross Reservoir, views of Forsythe Rocks
Difficulty: Easy
Topo map: Tungsten

Description

This riparian trail follows Forsythe Canyon Creek downhill through forests of pine, spruce, and Douglas-fir, with occasional stands of aspen. It skirts a "secret" waterfall and dead-ends at an inlet of Gross Reservoir. Wildflowers are spectacular in late May and June, but there's a lot of deadfall along the trail—a heavy infestation of spruce budworm has killed many of the Douglas-firs. This area is a critical range for elk in winter.

From the parking area, follow an old jeep road downhill a short distance to Forsythe Canyon Creek. Just before reaching the creek, the main jeep road curves to the right. Take the branch that curves left. Descend to the confluence of two streams, cross to the north side, and turn right onto the trail (the left fork goes to private property). Although the trail is not well marked (it is not an official Forest Service trail and so is not maintained), you will find your way to Gross Reservoir by following the creek downstream on the left side.

When you reach the waterfall, the trail becomes somewhat indistinct. The best route heads uphill to the left for a short distance, goes over a small hump, and then descends to the foot of the falls. There is also a faint trail that crosses the boulders just to the left of the falls, but this route involves some rock scrambling. From the waterfall, return to the main trail to the left to avoid raspberry briars and stickery brush. Continue downhill to the inlet of the reservoir.

History

Forsythe Canyon Creek is one of three major creeks draining into Gross Reservoir. The reservoir was built between 1952 and 1954.

Connections

Although the main trail dead-ends at the inlet, rough trails lead to several fishing spots at the reservoir itself.

Access

From the Boulder Canyon Road, take Magnolia Road (CR 132) for 6.8 miles to CR 68. Turn left and continue on CR 68 for 2.1 miles to Forest Service Road 359, on your right. If the barricade is up, park alongside the road; otherwise, turn onto FS 359 and park in the open area at the beginning of the jeep road.

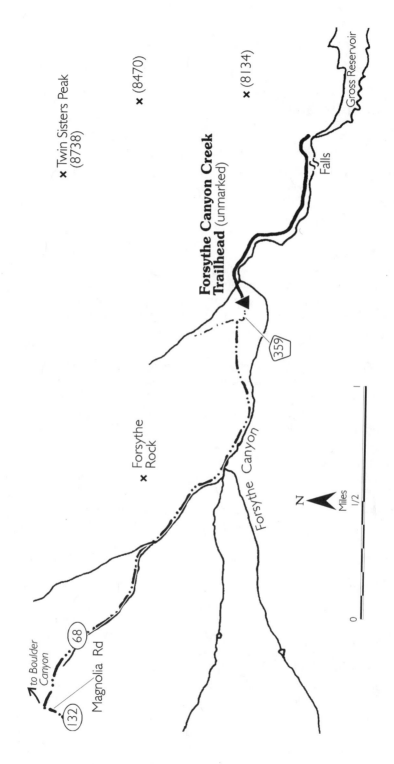

Forsythe Canyon Creek

Map labels:
- to Boulder Canyon
- 132
- 68
- Magnolia Rd
- **x** Forsythe Rock
- **x** Twin Sisters Peak (8738)
- **x** (8470)
- **x** (8134)
- **Forsythe Canyon Creek Trailhead** (unmarked)
- 359
- Forsythe Canyon
- Falls
- Gross Reservoir
- N
- Miles
- 0
- 1/2
- 1

Foothills Trail

Distance: 2.8 miles (one way from Foothills Nature Center to US 36)
Elevation: 5,500 to 5,533 feet
Highlights: Wonderland Lake, Hogback Ridge, views of plains and foothills, wildflowers and native grasses, birding
Difficulty: Easy
Topo map: Boulder

Description

This area consists of rolling grasslands and a burned-over hogback. The shale ridges are especially good for early wildflowers, and prairie dog colonies attract raptors and other predators such as coyotes. Occasionally, mountain lions are seen. Steer clear of the several unmarked paths that lead off from the main hiking trails; the main trails are well marked and easy to follow.

Although there are many possible starting points, this description begins at the Foothills Nature Center Trailhead on the south side of the center. The trail heads west, skirting the north side of Wonderland Lake, which is a wildlife refuge. Just beyond the lake, turn north and continue across grasslands for another 0.5 mile to a fork at the **Old Kiln Trail,** which branches off to the left and dead-ends at a water tank in 0.7 mile. Take the right fork and cross Lee Hill Road in 0.3 mile. Continue north and west for 0.8 mile to another junction. The right fork heads downhill 0.7 mile to the Foothills Trailhead on US 36. The left fork heads uphill to the **Hogback Ridge Loop.** This 1.7-mile loop climbs to 6,300 feet and is well worth a detour, as the views and flowers are excellent. A short distance below this loop, another trail heads north on an old railroad grade toward the former Beech Aircraft facilities.

History

Before you drop down to the Foothills Trailhead, look for an old game drive wall to the north of the trail. What looks like a crooked rock wall was used by early ("pre-horse," or pre-1550) Native Americans. Hunters would hide in blinds near the ridge top while others "drove" the game up the hill. Even a very low wall was sufficient to direct the animals toward the waiting hunters. Partway up the hill, the grading for the Boulder, Left Hand, and Middle Park Railroad cut through a portion of the wall in the 1880s. Although the railroad, which was projected to extend over Buchanan Pass, was not built, the grading is still visible.

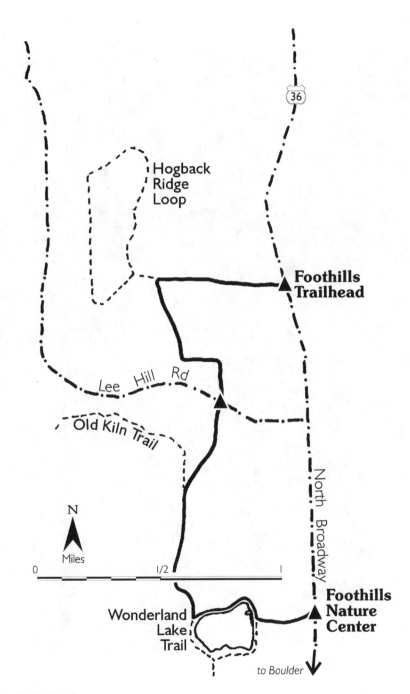

Foothills Trail

Game drive wall along Foothills Trail

A lime burning kiln, one of several that produced lime for the cement used to construct early Boulder buildings, can still be seen on the Old Kiln Trail just before reaching Lee Hill Road.

The 1990 Olde Stage fire destroyed several houses and burned out of control across the hogback, nearly reaching US 36. The fire was started by a burning mattress thrown from a window. Observing regeneration here is quite interesting.

Connections

Because of multiple trailheads and trail junctions, several loops or car shuttles are possible. Hikes can be extended by taking either of the connecting trails mentioned previously. The Foothills Trail also connects to the trail system at **Boulder Valley Ranch** (see page 12).

Access

Trail access points are located at the Foothills Nature Center (4201 North Broadway); the Foothills Trailhead, 0.4 mile north of the intersection of US 36 and North Broadway; Four Mile Creek Trailhead on Lee Hill Road, 0.5 mile west of North Broadway; and at Wonderland Lake Park at Poplar Avenue and Quince Circle.

Betasso Preserve: Canyon Loop Trail

Distance: 2.7 miles round-trip
Elevation: Starts at 6,480 feet, with a 460-foot loss and gain
Highlights: Ponderosa pine forest, woodland birds, Abert's squirrels, views of the plains
Difficulty: Easy to moderate
Topo map: Boulder

Description

From the east end of the Betasso loop road, the Canyon Loop Trail drops for about one mile through ponderosa pine forest and Douglas-fir in the moist ravines. After crossing a small, seasonal stream, the trail climbs back up through the forest into grassy meadows and joins an old fire road. Turn left (south) on this road, which leads past an old plum orchard, probably planted by Ronald McDonald who homesteaded here in 1922, and past the ruins of the McDonald Cabin in a meadow below the trail.

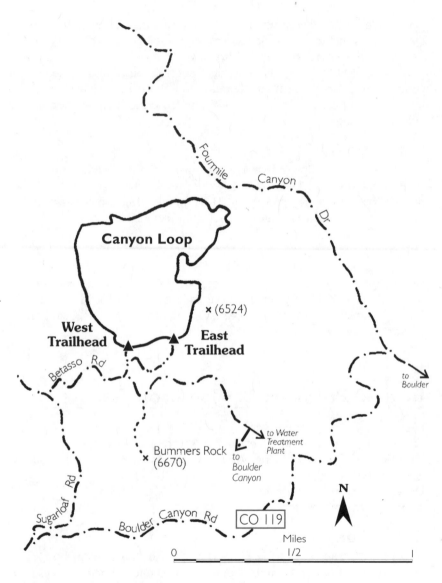

Canyon Loop

× (6524)

**West
Trailhead**

**East
Trailhead**

Fourmile Canyon Dr.

to
Boulder

Betasso Rd.

to Water
Treatment
Plant

Bummers Rock
× (6670)

to
Boulder
Canyon

Sugarloaf Rd.

Boulder Canyon Rd.

CO 119

N

Miles

0   1/2   1

Betasso Preserve: Canyon Loop Trail

Homestead ruins in the Betasso Preserve

When the fire road joins the Betasso loop road, turn left and return to the parking and picnic area. A slight detour near the road intersection leads up to some old farm machinery. On a hot day, you may find this trail more pleasant when done in reverse, taking advantage of the dense forest shade on the north-facing slopes for the uphill stretch.

History

The Blanchard family was the first to homestead the area, starting in 1912. They sold the ranch to Steve Betasso in 1915. The Betassos raised cattle here until 1976, when Ernie Betasso sold it to Boulder County to preserve the land.

Connections

Bummers Rock Trail takes off from the section of the Betasso Road that leads to the Boulder Filtration Plant. This trail (0.5 mile round-trip) goes to a lookout point and is a good place to see Boulder Creek granodiorite, igneous rock dated at 1.7 billion years old. A mountain-biking link built in 2001 connects Betasso and Boulder Canyon. Mountain bikes are banned, however, on the Canyon Loop Trail on Wednesdays and Saturdays and on Bummers Rock Trail at all times. Phone (303) 441-4559 for current regulations.

Access

From Boulder Canyon, turn north on Sugarloaf Road and go 0.8 mile. Turn right at the sign for the Betasso Filtration Plant and go another half-mile to where the road forks. The left fork goes to a picnic area and trailheads, the right fork to Bummers Rock Trailhead and the Betasso Filtration Plant.

Mount Sanitas Loop

Distance: 3.1 miles round-trip
Elevation: 5,520 to 6,863 feet
Highlights: Brilliantly colored sandstone formations, views of peaks and plains, wildflowers, wildlife
Difficulty: Moderate to difficult
Topo map: Boulder

Description

From the parking area at the mouth of Sunshine Canyon, walk behind the picnic pavilion, cross the bridge over the creek, and turn left at the Mount Sanitas sign. Follow the steep trail on the west side of the reddish sandstone formations, which are popular with rock climbers. The trail continues to climb steeply past enormous lichen-encrusted boulders that have eroded into strange shapes and through ponderosa pines to culminate in 1.5 miles at one of the best overlooks of the city of Boulder. About halfway to the summit, the trail follows a ridge with views of snowcapped peaks to the west, the plains to the east, and Bear Peak and the Flatirons to the south. Because of the rapid elevation gain, you see wildflowers at vastly different stages of development in spring. Look for raptors and listen for canyon wrens. Watch out for dog poop!

You can return the way you came up or, to complete the loop, take the **East Ridge Trail** 1.8 miles. This trail drops steeply down from the northeast side of the summit. It winds past sandstone slabs, passes several quarries, and joins the **Sanitas Valley Trail**—an old fire road that was once a wagon road to the quarries. Turn right (south) on the road, which leads back through a grassy valley and returns to the parking area.

Because of loose gravel on the steep portions of the trail, good boots are recommended.

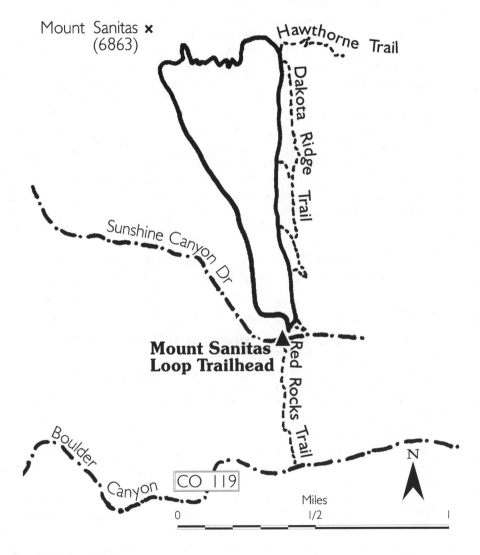

Mount Sanitas ✗
(6863)

Hawthorne Trail

Dakota Ridge Trail

Sunshine Canyon Dr

**Mount Sanitas
Loop Trailhead**

Red Rocks Trail

Boulder

Canyon

CO 119

N

Miles
0   1/2   1

Mount Sanitas Loop

History

The mountain takes its name from the Colorado, or Boulder, Sanitarium, built in 1895 by Seventh-Day Adventists, which preceded the present-day Mapleton Center. Some of the first hikers on Mount Sanitas were probably tuberculosis patients who came to Boulder for the good air.

Sandstone from the quarries, operated by the University of Colorado during the 1920s, was used in many campus buildings, such as Sewall Hall.

Connections

The **Dakota Ridge Trail** branches to the east of the **Sanitas Valley Trail** and meanders for 0.9 mile along the hogback east of Mount Sanitas. The 0.4-mile **Hawthorne Trail** is a spur connecting this trail system to Hawthorn Avenue. The trail to **Red Rocks and Anemone Hill** (see next trail description) is on the south side of Sunshine Canyon and a short distance west.

Access

The trailhead is at the mouth of Sunshine Canyon, west of Boulder Community Hospital's Mapleton Center at Mapleton Avenue and 4th Street.

Red Rocks and Anemone Hill Trail Loop

Distance: 2 miles round-trip
Elevation: 5,440 to 6,040 feet
Highlights: Spectacular red sandstone formations, early blooming spring flowers, historical site
Difficulty: Easy to moderate
Topo map: Boulder

Description

From Settlers Park on West Pearl Street, follow the trail that goes uphill to the east side of the Red Rocks formation. Because this is a heavily used area, please stay on the designated trail.

Circle the rocks on the east side for views across the city. From the highest point on the trail, take the left hand fork, circling the north end of the rock formation. (A spur trail on the north side of the rocks and some rock scrambling will take you to the top of the formation.) The trail drops to a grassy saddle above the abandoned site of Sunshine Reservoir. At the

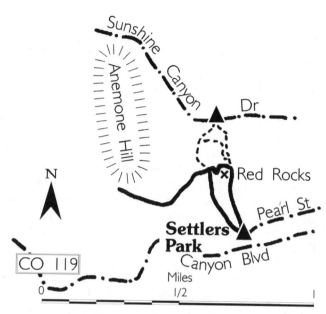

Red Rocks and Anemone Hill Loop

four-way intersection you can look down into Sunshine Canyon to the north and Boulder Canyon to the south. A depression between the saddle and Boulder Canyon is all that remains of Red Rocks Reservoir, Boulder's first reservoir, completed in 1876 and abandoned in 1906. The larger depression between the saddle and Sunshine Canyon held Sunshine Reservoir, Boulder's second water storage facility built in 1891 and abandoned in the 1950s. Both were fed by Boulder Creek. The Sunshine Hydroelectric Facility, built in 1986, is just above the old Sunshine Reservoir.

From the saddle, continue uphill to the southwest. The trail ascends up the south side of Anemone Hill, named for the pasqueflowers that were once abundant here. The official trail ends at the aqueduct where Arapaho Peak suddenly looms into view.

Retrace your route back down Anemone Trail. When you return to the grassy saddle, take the trail to the south, which descends to Settlers Park and avoids the climb back up to the Red Rocks. When you return to the grassy saddle, take the trail to the south, which descends to Settlers Park and avoids the climb back up to the Red Rocks.

History

The first settlers in Boulder County were goldseekers from Nebraska, led here by Thomas A. Aikins. They camped near the Red Rocks. Uncertainty exists regarding the exact date of their arrival. October 17, 1858, was long accepted as the arrival date of the first settlers, based on an account written in 1880 by Amos Bixby. However, historian Tom Meier has done extensive research into letters and newspaper accounts written at the time of settlement and believes the party could not have arrived before December 21, 1858. Accounts also vary regarding the number and names of the first settlers.

Several irrigation ditches built in the 1880s cut across this area. In the early 1900s, Frederick Law Olmsted recommended that the Red Rocks become a public park and called the city irrigation ditches "a veritable treasure of municipal decoration" that should be incorporated into "promenades."

Connections

From the Pearl Street parking area, follow the sidewalk through the underpass beneath Canyon Boulevard to Eben G. Fine Park, where you can continue on the **Boulder Creek Path** (see page 25). If you continue north past the Red Rocks to Sunshine Canyon, you can cross the road to the trailhead for **Mount Sanitas** (see page 68).

Access

Start from Settlers Park at the west end of Pearl Street. You can also do this trail "backwards" by starting from the trailhead on the south side of Sunshine Canyon, almost directly across from Mount Sanitas, and taking the old service road up to the grassy saddle.

This trail is especially lovely in spring because of the many early blooming flowers along the irrigation ditches. We have seen phlox, flax, thimbleberry, evening primrose, spiderwort, and geraniums as early as April. Brush-loving birds, such as towhees and thrushes, also like to hide out in the wild plums and other shrubbery along the ditches. Several years ago a varied thrush (rare in Colorado) was observed here.

Flagstaff Trail

Distance: 1.5 miles one way
Elevation: 5,720 to 6,820 feet
Highlights: Flagstaff Summit with views of the plains and city, ponderosa pine forest, wildlife, wildflowers

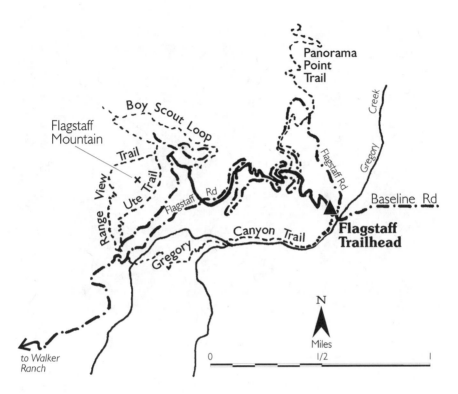

Flagstaff Trail

Difficulty: Moderate
Topo map: Boulder, Eldorado Springs

Description

Although this trail takes you across busy Flagstaff Road five times, it does lead you to the top of Flagstaff Mountain, one of Boulder's best known landmarks. Because most of the views are to the east, the trail is good for sunrise and moonrise walks. The long straight line that stretches east, seemingly to infinity, is Baseline Road. It marks the fortieth parallel, and is historically important because it once divided Nebraska Territory (a free state) from Kansas Territory (a slave state). The fortieth parallel still marks the boundary between those two states today.

The rather steep trail starts on the left side of Flagstaff Road at the turnoff for Gregory Canyon Trailhead. The trail culminates just below the top of Flagstaff Mountain, across the road from an old well. The unmarked

Company along the Flagstaff Trail

summit of the mountain (6,872 feet) is just south of the picnic area and about sixty additional feet in elevation gain. Along Flagstaff Trail several side trails lead to popular rock climbs and viewpoints, but the main trail is always obvious. Spring and summer wildflowers are magnificent, and deer, squirrels, chipmunks, and birds are abundant. On summer weekends, stop to see the nature displays at the Flagstaff Summit Center, where volunteers answer questions about local natural history.

History

Around 1910, there was talk of building an amusement park on top of Flagstaff Mountain, to be reached by an inclined railway. Landscape architect Frederick Law Olmsted objected: "The scenery of Flagstaff Mountain is too noble, too magnificent, too precious to be wasted in serving as an almost unneeded accompaniment to the fun of roller coasters, moving pictures and vaudeville shows." He urged that it be left as "a place of quiet mountain scenery, remote and vast, where the weary can find peace."

The Civilian Conservation Corps, created by Franklin Delano Roosevelt during the Great Depression, made a significant contribution to the beautification and preservation of Flagstaff Mountain. Among other projects, they built 25 miles of trails, improved Flagstaff Road, constructed Chapman Drive (a back road down Flagstaff, now closed to traffic), and built the Sunrise Circle Amphitheater on the east side of the summit—a site often used for weddings, religious services, and community events.

Several stories exist explaining the name "Flagstaff." According to Martin Parsons, a park ranger in 1916 who patrolled the area on horseback, two men got into an argument. One man lost his shirt, and the victor tied it to the top of a dead pine tree visible from the city. From the turn of the century to 1947, flag contests were held annually by students from the Boulder Preparatory School. The "Onies" (freshmen) had two hours to plant a flag on the mountain while the "Toots" (sophomores) tried to wrest it from them. These competitions were discontinued in 1947 because of some students' injuries.

The first United States flag was officially flown on Flagstaff Mountain on June 1, 1918. It was a wooden flag. Weddings held at the amphitheater date back as early as 1917.

Connections

At the summit, connections can be made with the **Range View Trail** (see page 76) or the **Ute Trail.** For a loop hike, take either of these trails down to Realization Point, cross Flagstaff Road and continue past the sign for Green Mountain Lodge. In a short distance this trail forks and the left branch becomes the **Gregory Canyon Trail** (see page 77), which leads to Baird Park at the bottom. The **Panorama Point Trail** starts at 3rd Street and Arapahoe Avenue and joins the Flagstaff Trail near Panorama Point. The **Boy Scout Trail,** which connects the Sunrise Circle Amphitheater with the spur to Artists Point, can be joined from several points on top of Flagstaff Mountain.

Access

At the spot where Baseline Road becomes Flagstaff Road, turn left onto a dirt road that promptly dead-ends at Gregory Canyon Trailhead in Baird Park. Walk back down the dirt road to the Flagstaff Trailhead. Or, you can park alongside the road near the Flagstaff Trailhead, if there is space.

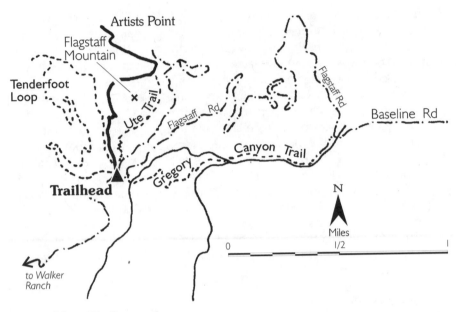

Range View Trail

Range View Trail

Distance: 0.6 mile one way
Elevation: 6,748 to 6,800 feet
Highlights: Views of the Indian Peaks
Difficulty: Easy
Topo map: Boulder, Eldorado Springs

Description

Most foothills trails provide "windows" through which we can peek at the Indian Peaks, but Range View Trail from Flagstaff Road to Artists Point offers one continuous view. The coniferous forest you pass through provides habitat for Abert's squirrels, blue grouse, crossbills, and other conifer-loving creatures but does not block the view.

From Realization Point, the trail climbs up the west side of Flagstaff Mountain. At the summit the trail connects with the Boy Scout Trail and goes along a dirt road for a short distance to Artists Point, where a short spur leads northwest to Mays Point.

Connections

The **Tenderfoot Loop** (2.5 miles) branches to the left almost immediately beyond the Range View Trailhead and goes downhill. You can return to Realization Point from the summit of Flagstaff via the **Ute Trail.** A
row of ponderosa pines marks a section of this trail that was used by the
Utes, possibly from as far back as the sixteenth century. The pines grow in
the rutted trail in an almost perfect row about 100 feet long. Across the
road from Realization Point, you can join the **Gregory Canyon Trail** (see
next trail description) or the **Greenman** and **Ranger Trails** (see page 81).

Access

Park at Realization Point 3.4 miles up Flagstaff Road, where the road
intersects with Chapman Drive.

Gregory Canyon

Distance: 1.1 miles one way
Elevation: 5,800 to 6,680 feet
Highlights: Wildflowers, brush-loving birds, red rock formations, stream-
side habitat
Difficulty: Moderate
Topo map: Eldorado Springs

Description

This short but steep trail climbs above Gregory Creek and offers views
of the edges of the Flatirons. In springtime, it's one of the best wildflower
hikes in the county. Apple and plum trees (and lots of poison ivy) are thick
at the beginning of the trail and give way to pine trees near the top. Listen
for canyon and rock wrens as well as other brush birds. Chipmunks and
golden-mantled ground squirrels are also common.

About halfway up, the trail crosses a side creek, ascends through
ponderosa pines to a grassy meadow, and ends at a dirt road across from
Realization Point where several trails diverge.

History

The canyon is named for John Gregory, an early gold miner who in
the 1860s built a road up the canyon to his mines at Black Hawk. This
canyon was the main route to Black Hawk for many years. Gregory's

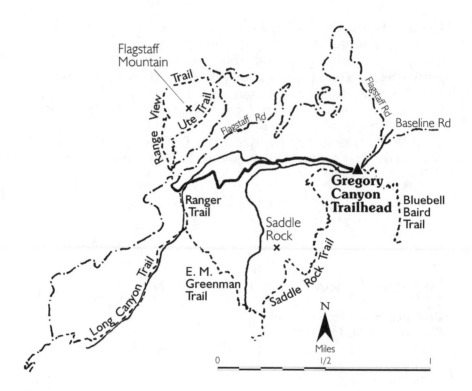

Gregory Canyon

"corduroy road" consisted of logs placed close together across the route and was almost impassable. Several other attempts were made to build a road up the canyon, and finally, in 1873, a rough road was built and used until Flagstaff Road was completed in 1906.

Many old apple trees along this trail and others were probably planted by Ernest Greenman, Boulder's local "Johnny Appleseed," or are descendants of his trees. On his many hiking treks, Greenman planted fruit seeds throughout the foothills. His niece, Dorothy Greenman, recalled that when they walked in the mountains, he carried seeds of all kinds in his pockets and scattered them around the springs.

Connections

At the top of the canyon, several other hiking possibilities open up. You can continue up **Green Mountain** (see page 81) or cross Flagstaff

Road to take either the **Range View** (see page 76) or **Ute Trails** to the summit of Flagstaff Mountain. If you wish to return to the trailhead via a different route, take the **Flagstaff Trail** (see page 72). The **Bluebell-Baird Trail** (see page 88) and the **Saddle Rock Trail** (see next trail description) also start from Gregory Canyon Trailhead.

Access

At the spot where Baseline Road becomes Flagstaff Road, turn left onto a dirt road that promptly dead-ends at Gregory Canyon Trailhead in Baird Park. The Gregory Canyon Trail begins to the left of the outhouse.

Saddle Rock

Distance: 1.3 miles one way
Elevation: 5,800 to 7,050 feet
Highlights: Red rock formations, dense coniferous forest
Difficulty: Moderate to strenuous
Topo map: Eldorado Springs

Description

This short but steep trail provides a good workout in pleasant surroundings and leads to a prominent rock formation. It starts together with the **Gregory Canyon Trail** (see page 77) but almost immediately forks to the left, crosses Gregory Creek, and heads uphill through a dense Douglas-fir and ponderosa pine forest, following a tributary of Gregory Creek. Shortly after leaving this tributary, the trail joins the **Amphitheater Trail**. (For a short loop, you can turn left at this point and descend back to the trailhead.)

The Saddle Rock Trail continues to zigzag up to another junction. The left branch goes to the First Flatiron, and the right branch enters a more open area with good views of the First Flatiron, edge on, and of the city of Boulder. Continue on the right branch. At this point you are almost to Saddle Rock. Although the aptly named formation is conspicuous from many points in the city, it's easy to miss from the trail, which actually passes above it. At the crest of the ridge where the Indian Peaks become visible, there are some rather insignificant rocks on the right. Saddle Rock is north of these rocks and is reached by a short, easy scramble.

Return via this same route until you reach the marked junction of the Amphitheater and Saddle Rock Trails. Continue down the Amphitheater

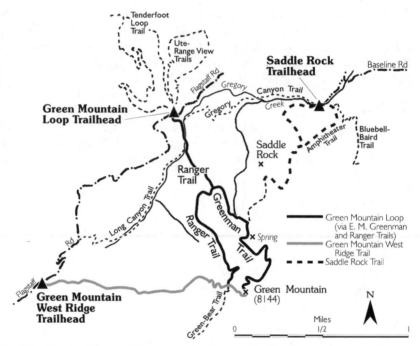

Saddle Rock, Green Mountain Loop via E. M. Greenman and
Ranger Trails, and Green Mountain West Ridge Trail

branch, which passes under a semicircle of sandstone formations called "the
Amphitheater," a popular area for rock climbing, to return to the trailhead.

History

The gulch that the trail follows, called Contact Canyon, contains remnants of old logging roads and was used for conditioning by skiers training
for the Olympics in the 1960s.

Connections

At Saddle Rock you can continue along the crest and drop down to the
E. M. Greenman Trail (see next trail description) and either return to the
trailhead via **Gregory Canyon** (see page 77) or climb Green Mountain via
the E. M. Greenman Trail. From the amphitheater, you can drop down to
join the **Bluebell-Baird Trail** (see page 88) just before reaching the Gregory Canyon Trailhead.

Access

At the spot where Baseline Road becomes Flagstaff Road, turn left onto a dirt road that promptly dead-ends at the Gregory Canyon Trailhead in Baird Park. Both the Saddle Rock and the Gregory Canyon Trails begin to the left of the outhouse.

Green Mountain Loop via E. M. Greenman and Ranger Trails

(See map on page 80)

Distance: 3.3 miles round-trip
Elevation: 6,748 to 8,144 feet
Highlights: Views of peaks and plains from the top, coniferous forest habitat, ladybugs on summit
Difficulty: Moderate
Topo map: Eldorado Springs

Description

From the west end of the parking area, walk a short distance down the dirt road (past the sign that says "Green Mountain Lodge") to a small meadow. Turn right and follow the old road to the lodge. A sign for the Ranger Trail is on the left side of the lodge. Follow this trail up through a moist, coniferous forest thick with bracken fern, moss, and various species of wintergreen. Several unusual plants, including rare orchids, grow on the north slopes of this mountain, and numerous species of butterflies nectar on the flowers in the meadow below the lodge.

In 0.3 mile the Ranger Trail forks to the right. Turn left onto the Greenman Trail, which contours into another gulch and is soon joined by the **Saddle Rock Trail**; both junctions are well marked. Shortly after the Saddle Rock sign, Greenman Trail crosses a small stream (Greenman Springs, built by Ernest Greenman, is just above the trail at this point) and begins to climb steeply, making numerous switchbacks up to the Green Mountain summit. A viewfinder identifies the peaks from Mount Evans to Longs Peak, and in autumn and early spring ladybugs by the thousands congregate here.

From the summit, drop down to the west on the **Green Mountain West Ridge Trail** (see page 83). Very soon the Ranger Trail branches to the right and drops steeply via switchbacks to the junction with Greenman Trail, ending at Green Mountain Lodge.

Green Mountain Lodge after a heavy snow

History

This trail is named for Ernest Greenman, who came to Boulder in 1896. He worked as a surveyor on the narrow gauge railroad from Sunset to Glacier Lake, was one of the founders of the Rocky Mountain Climbers Club, and planted hundreds of apple trees throughout the canyons of Boulder's foothills. He led more than one hundred climbs of the Third Flatiron and more than thirty trips to Arapaho Peak. His photo collection, stored in the Carnegie Library in Boulder, shows climbers standing atop Longs and other local peaks and picnicking at the Flatirons. According to Greenman, a trail existed on Green Mountain "as far back as 1917."

The Ranger Trail was probably built by Martin Parsons, an early park ranger. The Civilian Conservation Corps built Green Mountain Lodge (sometimes called the Boy Scout Cabin) in the 1930s for hiking clubs and other organizations.

Connections

For a longer hike, you can take the **Gregory Canyon Trail** (see page 77) to its junction with the Ranger Trail, or the **Saddle Rock Trail** (see page 79) to its junction with the Greenman Trail. Across Flagstaff Road at Realization Point, you can connect with the **Range View** (see page 76), **Ute,** and **Tenderfoot Trails.** On the right side of Green Mountain Lodge, the **Long Canyon Trail** (1.1 miles) follows upper Gregory Creek, emerging on Flagstaff Road just south of Cathedral Park picnic area. If you use two cars, you can ascend the **Green Mountain West Ridge Trail** (see next trail description) and descend via either the Greenman or the Ranger Trails.

Access

Drive up Flagstaff Road 3.4 miles to a three-way intersection and park in the area to the left, opposite Realization Point.

Green Mountain West Ridge Trail

(See map on page 80)

Distance: 1.4 miles one way
Elevation: 7,544 to 8,144 feet
Highlights: Views of snowcapped peaks, variety of bird species
Difficulty: Easy
Topo map: Eldorado Springs

Description

This trail is the shortest, easiest route up Green Mountain, but its chief blessing is an almost continuous, unobstructed view of the Front Range to the west. The trail is also snow-free much earlier in the spring than either the Greenman or the Ranger Trails.

From the trailhead, the trail goes gently down and up, down and up. Just before the final, rather steep ascent you cross a trail junction: the **Ranger Trail** descends to the left, and the **Green Bear Trail** heads to the right (southwest) to Bear Canyon.

Connections

From the summit you can descend via the **Greenman** or the **Ranger Trail** (see page 81), or make a loop returning to Green Mountain West Ridge. This balloon shaped route is fairly steep with about 2,000 feet of elevation loss and gain. An easier hike is to use two cars, leaving one at Realization Point and descending to it from the summit.

Access

At Realization Point, 3.4 miles up Flagstaff Road, turn left and drive 1.6 miles, past Cathedral Park Picnic Area, to the trailhead on the east side of the road. Roadside parking is available but be careful not to block private drives.

Mesa Trail

Distance: 6.1 miles one way
Elevation: 5,680 to 5,600 feet (north to south), with many ups and downs
Highlights: Views of the Flatirons and other rock formations, a variety of habitats, wildflowers, wildlife, and access to many other trails
Difficulty: Moderate
Topo map: Eldorado Springs

Description

Because this trail goes through habitats ranging from ponderosa pine forests to grasslands to wetlands, the variety of wildflowers and wildlife is exceptional, even though there is little elevation change. Deer are abundant, and black bears, coyotes, foxes, and mountain lions are sometimes sighted. Golden eagles and prairie falcons nest in the cliffs and, in 1991, peregrine falcons returned to nest near the Flatirons after an absence of over thirty-five years.

There is a slight overall elevation loss if you start on the north end at the Chautauqua Park parking area. Walk 0.6 mile up the paved old Bluebell Road (closed to traffic) to the outhouse just below the Bluebell Shelter, for an elevation gain of about 300 feet. The Mesa Trail begins to the left of the outhouse and goes up and down hill, across mesas and into canyons, and ends at the South Mesa Trailhead on Eldorado Springs Drive. (Because of the many small ups and downs, the hike adds up to about 1400 total feet of elevation gain.) From north to south, you pass the mouths of six major canyons. Lateral trails drop down Bluebell, Shanahan, and Skunk Canyons and head up Bear, Fern, and Shadow Canyons. You hike below such well known rock formations as the Flatirons, Seal Rock, Devils Thumb, the Maiden, and the Matron.

Much of the trail consists of old, connecting roads, and occasionally a road remnant heading off to the left or right will lead to an abandoned cabin, stone quarry, or up a side canyon. However, the Mesa Trail and its laterals (several of which are described later) are well marked, so it's hard to get lost. The main trail heads in a generally southerly direction until it reaches the dirt road below Shadow Canyon. At this point, turn east (left) and follow the road for 0.9 mile down to the South Mesa Trailhead.

You can hike this trail from either direction, you can pick it up at several different points, and you can do various loops and figure eights on the Mesa Trail network.

History

When Boulder mountaineer Ernest Greenman was in his eighties, Cleve McCarty published his reminiscences in *High over Boulder*. Greenman remembered working with the Rocky Mountain Climber's Club and the Boulder Chamber of Commerce to place two hundred cairns between Boulder and Eldorado Springs: "We blazed trees, trimmed limbs, and made a little trail clear across there in '24...might have been in the spring of '25."

Long before this, however, there had been primitive toll roads and quarry roads that were later incorporated into the trail. The remains of the Wood-Bergheim Quarry is a short distance above the junction of the Mesa and Enchanted Mesa Trails, and the old Anderson quarry, which supplied stone for the historic Boulder Depot, is at the entrance to Skunk Canyon.

There are also remains of several cabins and buildings along the trail. The tiny stone hut just south of the turnoff to the Wood-Bergheim Quarry was built in 1935 by Harriet (Harmon) and Frank Roosa on the Harmon Ranch and is still an inholding owned by the Roosa Family. The story that it was a shelter for a girl riding horseback to and from school at the turn of the century is, sadly, just a legend. Near the south end of the Mesa Trail, you'll find domestic iris still growing near a fallen-down wooden shack called "the Schoolmarm's Cabin." According to Dock Teegarden, who has unearthed a wealth of local history, the cabin was used by Miss Florence Lane, a red-headed Denver schoolteacher who drove her Model T Ford up the road for weekend and summer retreats in the 1920s and 1930s. There also may have been an older building on the site.

In the 1970s, the City of Boulder rerouted the southern part of the trail that now ends just beyond the historic Doudy-Debacker-Dunn House.

Connections

From the Bluebell Shelter you can take the **Bluebell-Baird Trail** (see page 88), which connects to the **Gregory Canyon Trail** (see page 77). Several other trails branch off from Bluebell-Baird. From the south end of the Mesa Trail, you can cross Eldorado Springs Drive and continue on **Doudy**

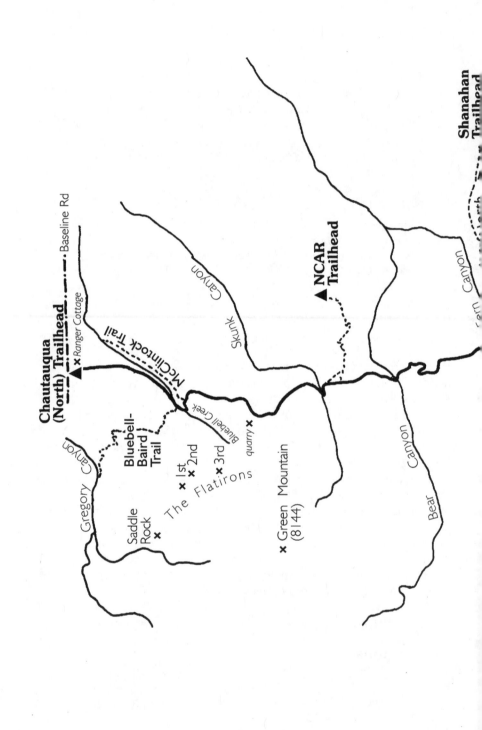

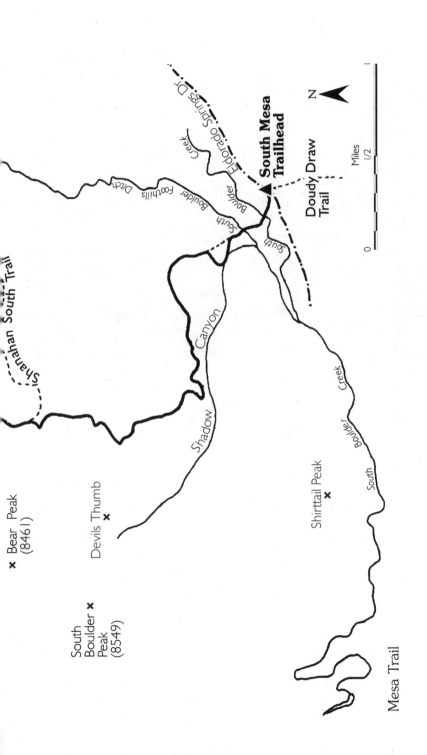

× Bear Peak
(8461)

South
Boulder × Peak
(8549)

Devils Thumb ×

Shanahan South Trail

Foothills Ditch

South Boulder Creek

Eldorado Springs Dr.

South Mesa
Trailhead

Doudy Draw
Trail

Canyon

Shadow

Shirttail Peak
×

South Boulder Creek

Mesa Trail

N

Miles

0   1/2   1

Taking a break along the Mesa Trail

Draw Trail (see page 110). There are numerous lateral trails to the Mesa Trail, many of which are described elsewhere in this section of the book.

Access

The two main access points are at Chautauqua Park (the turnoff is 1 block west of 9th Street off of Baseline Road) and the South Mesa Trailhead on Eldorado Springs Drive, 2 miles west of SR 93. There are several other access points, including the National Center for Atmospheric Research (NCAR), Shanahan Trail, or McClintock Trail. Check a trail map, such as the *Colorado Mountain Club Trail Map: Boulder Mountain Parks and Nearby Open Space,* for other possibilities.

Bluebell-Baird Trail

Distance: 0.7 mile one way
Elevation: 5,800 to 6,000 feet
Highlights: Ponderosa pines, spring wildflowers, colorful fall shrubs

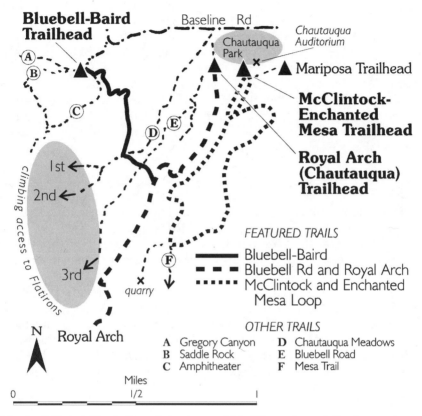

Bluebell-Baird Trail, Royal Arch, and McClintock and Enchanted
Mesa Loop

Difficulty: Easy
Topo map: Eldorado Springs

Description

Starting at the south side of Baird Park, this trail crosses Gregory
Creek, diverges from the **Amphitheater Trail,** climbs slightly through a
meadow filled with native grasses, continues through a ponderosa pine forest, and ends at Bluebell Shelter. Bluebell-Baird serves primarily as an access trail to several other trails. However, about halfway along the trail in
autumn, a red sumac patch frames an outstanding view of the First Flatiron
and, in spring, some of the best stands of coralroot orchids grow here.

History

The trail and the park are named for Dr. and Mrs. William Baird, who donated 160 acres in Gregory Canyon to the city in 1908. In the 1930s, the Civilian Conservation Corps built a trail connecting Gregory Canyon with Bluebell Canyon. In 1948, Harris Thompson built a 200-foot rope tow (later extended another 850 feet uphill), powered by a Dodge gasoline engine. He and Steve Bradley, University of Colorado ski coach, operated the "Mesa Ski Slope" for a few seasons. You can still see the grass-covered mound that served as a ski jump.

Connections

Very soon after the trail crosses the creek, the **Amphitheater Trail** branches to the right and climbs to the Amphitheater, a favorite rock climbing area, and on up to join the **Saddle Rock Trail** (see page 79). Soon after this junction, the **Chautauqua Trail** branches to the left, crosses just east of the former site of the Mesa Ski Slope, and terminates at Chautauqua Park.

Just before you reach the Bluebell Shelter, a trail to the **First** and **Second Flatirons** branches to the right. At the Bluebell Shelter you can follow Bluebell Road to the **Mesa Trail** (see page 84) or take any of the other trails, such as the **Royal Arch** trail (see below), that radiate from this point. To make a loop trip, walk down the road and take either the **Bluebell Mesa** or the **Chautauqua Trails** back up to the Bluebell-Baird Trail.

Access

Turn left onto a dirt road at the point where Baseline Road becomes Flagstaff Road. The road promptly dead-ends at a small parking area at the Gregory Canyon Trailhead in Baird Park.

Royal Arch

(See map on page 89)

Distance: 1.5 miles one way
Elevation: 5,680 to 6,950 feet
Highlights: Large sandstone arch, views of the plains and of flatiron formations, coniferous forest habitat
Difficulty: Moderate
Topo map: Eldorado Springs

Royal Arch

Description

This is a short and steep trail that frequently ascends via stone "stairs" or log risers. The reward at the end is a twenty-foot sandstone arch framing views of Boulder Valley to the southeast and red rock formations to the north.

From the Chautauqua Park parking lot, walk 0.6 mile up the paved old Bluebell Road (closed to traffic) to Bluebell Shelter. The Royal Arch Trail begins together with the Third Flatirons Trail, just above the shelter. Just beyond the sign, the Arch Trail veers to the left and continues through a ponderosa pine forest. After crossing Bluebell Creek, which is often dry, the trail zigzags uphill past a viewpoint at a rock outcropping and continues to a saddle, called Sentinel Pass. Here you'll have excellent views of the south face of the Third Flatiron and of the two "ironing boards." In spring, falcons and other raptors often nest in the Flatirons. Listen for their shrill cries as well as the cascading song of the canyon wrens.

At the saddle, the trail drops abruptly to the left for about one hundred feet into another gulch and then climbs very steeply up to the arch. When you come to a slot cave and a small spring, you are almost there.

History

For many years, this arch, which looks like two kissing marmots, was an annual goal for climbers from Chautauqua. Early photos show ladies in long skirts and gentlemen in coats and ties resting beneath the window. According to Pat Ament and Cleve McCarty in *High over Boulder*, the arch was discovered by Lawrence Bass of Boulder, and the first trail to it was built about 1898 by "Rocky Mountain Joe" Sturtevant, an early Boulder photographer and hiking guide. It was named by Edwin Chamberlin, one of the founders of the Rocky Mountain Climber's Club, who was studying for his Masonic Royal Arch Degree at the time. The city purchased the land in 1920, and the present trail was built the following year by the Boulder Rotarians, with help from the Boy Scouts, Ernest Greenman, and Eben G. Fine.

Connections

Several other trails take off from the vicinity of Bluebell Shelter and can be tacked onto the Royal Arch Trail for a longer hike, including the **Bluebell-Baird Trail** (see page 88), **Mesa Trail** (see page 84), and the **Third Flatiron Trail,** which is chiefly an access trail for rock climbers and not described in this book.

Access

Start at Bluebell Shelter, approaching it either from the Mesa Trail North Trailhead at Chautauqua Park (see page 84) or from the Bluebell-Baird Trail at Baird Park (see page 88). Mileage given for this hike is determined from Chautauqua Park.

McClintock and Enchanted Mesa Loop

(See map on page 89)

Distance: 2.5 miles round-trip
Elevation: 5,730 to 6,160 feet
Highlights: Self-guided nature trail, wildflowers, brush-loving birds, deer
Difficulty: Easy
Topo map: Eldorado Springs

Description

This trail starts in plum and hawthorn thickets and climbs into an open, park-like forest of ponderosa pines where early spring pasqueflowers and spring beauties abound. The ponderosa pines are good places to look for Abert's squirrels.

From the picnic shelter south of Chautauqua Auditorium, the McClintock Trail descends to cross Bluebell Creek. Almost immediately it forks, with the left branch descending to Mariposa Avenue. Take the right branch that climbs to intersect the Enchanted Mesa Road at an old apple tree, which still bears crisp apples. Cross the road and continue uphill, paralleling Bluebell Creek. Interpretive signs explain the natural history of the area.

When the trail reaches the **Mesa Trail,** turn left (south) and continue 0.3 mile to a major trail intersection. The Mesa Trail continues straight ahead, and the right fork goes 0.3 mile to the abandoned Woods-Bergheim sandstone quarry. Take the left fork and go downhill past a covered city reservoir to the Enchanted Mesa Road, which is closed to traffic. This road intersects the McClintock Trail at Bluebell Creek. Return to Chautauqua Park via the McClintock Trail or the Enchanted Mesa Road. The road is very good for ski touring when there is sufficient snow.

History

"Save Enchanted Mesa" was the rallying cry for environmentalists when in the early 1960s the mesa was threatened by development. At that time it

became obvious that the Blue Line (a line above which the city would not provide water or sewer service) would not prevent development of the mountain
backdrop. Boulder citizens passed a bond issue to purchase the mesa.

The family of Henry H. McClintock, a former member of the Park
Board, provided the funds for interpretive plaques along the lower part of
this nature trail, named in his memory.

Connections

At its upper end, the McClintock Trail connects with the **Mesa Trail,**
which offers an array of hiking options (see page 84).

Access

Park near the Chautauqua Park picnic pavilion south of the Auditorium.
The turnoff for Chautauqua is 1 block west of 9th Street off of Baseline Road.

Walter Orr Roberts Nature Trail

Distance: 0.2 mile one way
Elevation: About 6,000 to 6,051 feet
Highlights: Views of Flatirons and plains, access to NCAR, deer, wild-
flowers, interpretive weather signs
Difficulty: Easy
Topo map: Eldorado Springs

Description

This wheelchair-accessible red-gravel trail around the plateau behind
the National Center for Atmospheric Research (NCAR) offers spectacular
views of the Flatirons. It's an ideal place to take out-of-town guests who
don't have much time or are not acclimated for hiking. To prevent erosion
caused by heavy use, please stay on the trail that starts on the northwest
side of NCAR and goes to the west end of Table Mountain Mesa.

Herds of mule deer can almost always be seen, and wildflowers are
spectacular in spring. Along the way, interpretive signs explain weather and
climate phenomena. When you read the "brown cloud" sign, look east to
observe the real thing. The award-winning NCAR building simulates the
pink sandstone of the Flatirons. Crushed Lyons sandstone was mixed with
the concrete to tint it pink. Inside, you can view additional exhibits on the
sun, atmospheric phenomena, climate, and the flora and fauna of the mesa
as well as changing art exhibits.

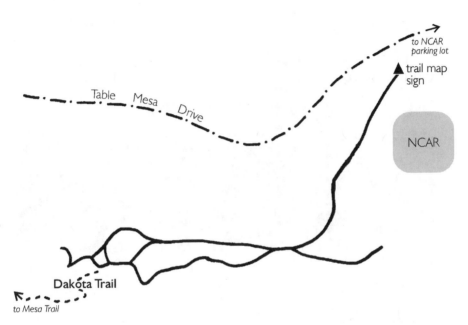

Walter Orr Roberts Nature Trail

History

This trail is named for Walter Orr Roberts, a conservationist and world-renowned physicist, who was instrumental in founding NCAR and securing its location in Boulder.

Connections

At the far end of the loop, the Dakota Trail connects NCAR to the **Mesa Trail** (see page 84) in about one-half mile. If you take this link, look for wild iris in late May in the dip before climbing to the water tank.

Access

Take Table Mesa Drive west to where it dead-ends at the NCAR parking lot. Public parking is permitted.

NCAR, near the Walter Orr Roberts Trailhead

Mallory Cave

Distance: 1.1 miles one way
Elevation: 6,080 to 7,020 feet
Highlights: One of few accessible caves in Boulder County, views of Boulder Valley, colorful rock slabs, bats
Difficulty: Moderate to strenuous (tricky rock scramble at end)
Topo map: Eldorado Springs

Description

Don't expect stalactites, stalagmites, or crystals in Mallory Cave. It's a fairly small, shallow, sandstone cave blackened by smoke, but since there are so few caves in the area, it's exciting to find.

The shortest approach is to take the Walter Orr Roberts Trail, starting on the west side of NCAR, and then the Dakota Trail, which crosses over the Dakota Formation to a water tank and then to the Mesa Trail. Turn south (left) on the Mesa Trail and very quickly you will see the Mallory Cave sign just north of Bear Canyon.

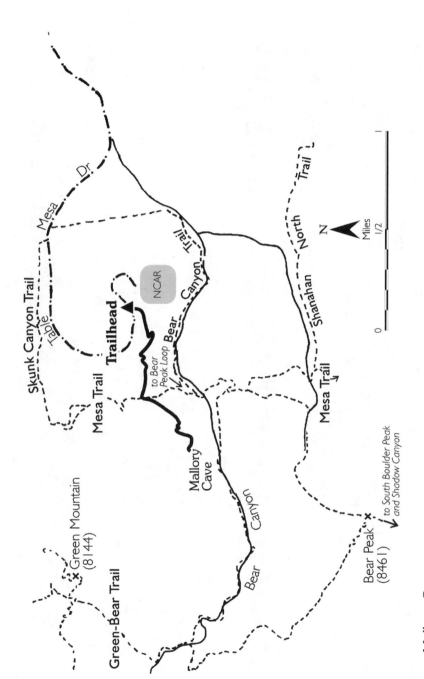

Mallory Cave

Views of NCAR and South Boulder from inside Mallory Cave

The Mallory Cave Trail climbs through Douglas-fir and ponderosa pine trees along the flank of Dinosaur Mountain. About halfway between the Mesa Trail and the cave, the trail goes up a stone "staircase" between slabs of pink sandstone. Eventually you come to a fork with a sign indicating the right branch goes to climbing rocks and the left branch to the cave. Beyond this sign you begin the final scramble up a slab and through a keyhole to the cave. There is mild exposure on the last fifty feet, but there are plenty of hand- and footholds so technical climbing skills are not needed. The stone tower above the cave is called Sharks Fin. In the summer many bats sleep upside down on the roof of the cave during the day. There are sometimes seasonal closings in summer and early fall to protect the Townsend's big-eared bats that use the cave.

History

Mallory Cave was discovered by E. C. Mallory in August, 1932, when he was eighteen years old and just out of the State Preparatory School. "I always wanted to explore where no one else went," he says. So one night his friend Martin Parsons, a longtime ranger in Boulder Mountain Parks, suggested the area on what is now Dinosaur Mountain. Mallory, on a solo hike, was searching for a trail through the ridges when he found the cave. Two huge stumps, obviously cut by saws, were in front of the cave. Parsons said that many years earlier two men cutting lumber had talked about a cave, but it was not recorded and so never found again. For many years Mallory kept the cave a secret except from Parsons and two other friends. Eventually, at Parsons' urging, he put up a sign saying "Rediscovered 1932 by E. C. Mallory." Mallory is a graduate of the University of Colorado and worked as a miner, in construction, and eventually as a chemist with the USGS.

Access

Park at NCAR at the very west end of Table Mesa Drive. Any access point for the Mesa Trail will also work.

Towhee and Homestead Loop

Distance: 2 miles round-trip
Elevation: 5,600 to 6,080 feet
Highlights: Ponderosa pine forests, brushy ravines, bird and animal watching, views of plains and foothills, historic buildings

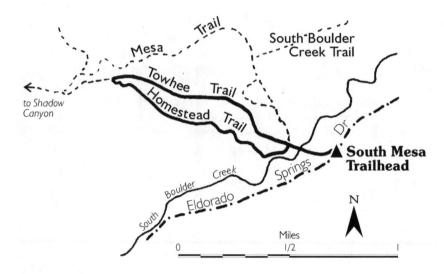

Towhee and Homestead Loop

Difficulty: Easy
Topo map: Eldorado Springs

Description

Although this trail is equally attractive from either starting point, this description starts with the Homestead section on the north side of the Doudy-Debacker-Dunn House. The Homestead Trail cuts behind an old apple orchard and follows South Boulder Creek for a short distance before heading up the open, south slope of a small ridge. When you think you have gained the top of the ridge, you are actually on a gentle plateau. The trail continues up through ponderosa pine forest and open grassy areas. Look for Abert's squirrels and mule deer. At the point where the plateau steepens rather sharply, the trail heads down the north side of the ridge, crosses Shadow Canyon Creek, and joins the Towhee Trail.

Turn right (east) on Towhee, which goes above the creek for a short distance before dropping down and crossing the creek again. Note that the creek may be dry in late summer and fall. The trail continues down, crosses a low stone wall and irrigation ditch, and ends back at the house. Look for marmots and chipmunks around the wall and for towhees and other brush birds in the chokecherries, hawthorns, and hackberries. In the spring, listen for boreal chorus frogs in the wet areas.

Doudy-Debacker-Dunn House

History

When Andrew Doudy first settled in the area around 1859, there were still traces of Native American camps, tepee rings, and arrowheads. Doudy, the first settler here, built a gristmill, sawmill, and a wooden house near South Boulder Creek. The flood of 1864 washed out the mills but not the house, which was purchased, along with the surrounding land, by John Debacker in 1869 for five hundred dollars. Debacker added the two-story stone house still standing on the site, and used water from an irrigation ditch to power a waterwheel that drove a cream separator and a washing machine.

In 1901, Debacker turned the property over to his daughter Emma and her husband, John Dunn, who raised dairy cattle here until John Dunn's death in 1953. The City of Boulder purchased the property in 1969 and demolished the wooden portion of the house for safety reasons. The stone walls in the area were built by out-of-work miners who, in the 1870s, removed rocks from Debacker's fields in exchange for food and lodging.

Connections

If you continue west at the junction of Homestead and Towhee Trails, you will rejoin the **Mesa Trail** (see page 84). If you keep heading west on the Mesa Trail, you will connect with the **Shadow Canyon Trail** (see page 106).

Access

Park at the South Mesa Trailhead on Eldorado Springs Drive 2 miles west of SR 93. Follow the Mesa Trail for approximately 0.1 mile to the Doudy-Debacker-Dunn House.

Big Bluestem and South Boulder Creek Loop

Distance: 4.3 miles (short loop), or 7.1 miles (long loop)
Elevation: 5,490 to 5,800 feet (short loop), or to 6200 feet (long loop)
Highlights: Native grasses, views of Flatiron formations
Difficulty: Easy to moderate
Topo map: Eldorado Springs, Louisville

Description

From the parking area at the pond, walk up Thomas Lane to where it dead-ends at a gate. Go through the gate and follow the trail uphill through fields of big bluestem and other native grasses, including switchgrass, Indian grass, and blue grama. (Incidentally, bluestem is also called "turkey foot" and is blue only in spring; in autumn, it's a cross between burgundy, peach, and mauve.)

In 2.3 miles you come to a junction where you must decide whether to take the short loop or the long loop. For the short loop, take the left fork to connect with the Mesa Trail in 0.1 mile. Turn left on the Mesa Trail and go another 0.1 mile to the South Boulder Creek Trail. Turn left again and follow this trail downhill to complete the loop. Near the end of the trail you pass a boggy area filled with cordgrass, a grass used by early settlers for roofing sod houses.

If you want to take the long loop, take the right fork, which heads up-hill past the ruins of an old homestead to connect with the Mesa Trail in 0.8 mile. Follow the Mesa Trail to the left for 0.4 mile. Take the first fork to the left, which heads downhill to connect with the South Boulder Creek Trail in 1.7 miles and completes the loop just previously described.

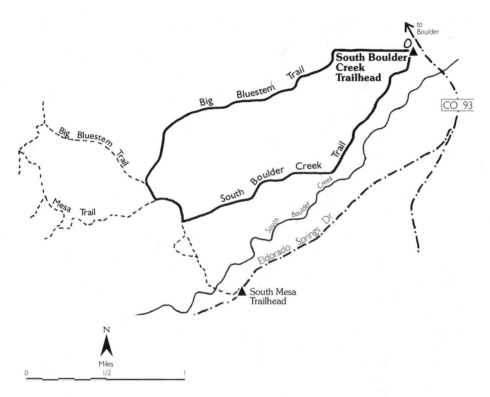

Big Bluestem and South Boulder Creek Loop

History

There were many homesteads in this area at the turn of the century, but most were abandoned between 1910 and 1920. Some of the ruins are still visible.

Connections

It's possible to continue on the **Mesa Trail** (see page 84) to either end if you do a car shuttle.

Access

Turn west off of SR 93 at Thomas Lane, 1.8 miles south of Table Mesa Drive. Immediately after turning, head into the parking lot for the South Boulder Creek Trailhead.

Bear Peak Loop via Bear Canyon, Bear Peak West Ridge, and Fern Canyon

Distance: 7.1 miles round-trip
Elevation: 6,080 to 8,461 feet
Highlights: Views of peaks and plains, cascading creek, lush canyons, rock slabs
Difficulty: Strenuous
Topo map: Eldorado Springs

Description

Bear Peak, with rounded shoulders and a pointed top, is one of Boulder's most prominent, familiar landmarks—visible throughout Boulder Valley. Several routes lead to the top, but this is one of the prettiest.

Take the Walter Orr Roberts Trail from the west side of NCAR to the Dakota Trail, which leads to a water tank and then to the Mesa Trail. Turn left (south) on the Mesa Trail, which soon drops to Bear Canyon Road (closed to traffic). Continue across Bear Creek and partway up the next hill where a sign points to Bear Canyon on your right (north). Follow the Bear Canyon Trail past a utility tower and continue uphill paralleling the creek, which the trail crosses numerous times. Poison ivy grows luxuriantly along the lower part of this trail along with wildflowers. Willows, cottonwoods, aspen, and flowering shrubs also grow along the creek bottom.

At 1.7 miles up the canyon, you come to a junction. Take the left fork up the Bear Peak West Ridge through a coniferous and scattered aspen forest. This ridge walk of 1.6 miles offers views of the Indian Peaks, Walker Ranch, a sawtooth ridge on Green Mountain, and the plains. Near the summit, the trail becomes quite steep, and there is a bit of a rock scramble at the top—but the view is worth it. In late spring and summer, swallows dart so near you can hear the swoosh of their wings.

Just below the summit, a sign points to the **Fern Canyon Trail,** which descends the northeast ridge to a fern-filled gulch where raptors often nest in the dramatic rock formations, such as Seal Rock. This trail is shorter than the route up but is extremely steep, losing over 2,000 feet of elevation in 1.2 miles. If you have knee problems, you may prefer to retrace your steps, taking the Bear Canyon route down. When the Fern Canyon Trail rejoins the Mesa Trail, turn left to complete the loop.

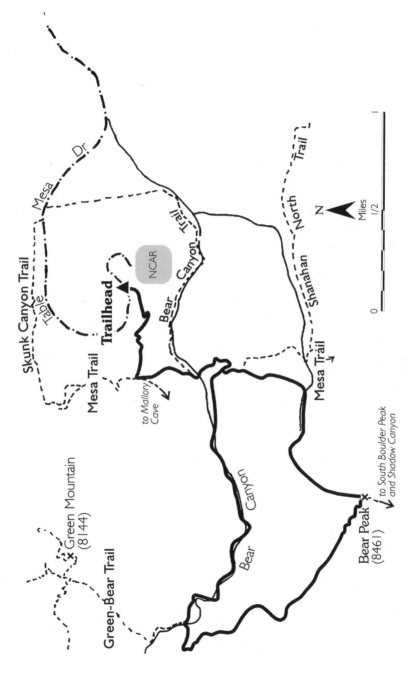

Bear Peak Loop via Bear Canyon, Bear Peak West Ridge, and Fern Canyon

Green Mountain
(8144)

Green-Bear Trail

Skunk Canyon Trail

Mesa Dr.

Table Mesa Trail

Mesa Trail

Trailhead

to Mallory Cave

NCAR

Bear Canyon Trail

Bear Canyon

Bear Peak
(8461)

to South Boulder Peak
and Shadow Canyon

Mesa Trail

Shanahan North Trail

N

Miles
0   1/2   1

History

In 1861, just three years after the first white encampment in Boulder, Henry Norton, a road builder, and George Williamson, a miner, built a wagon road up Bear Canyon to Black Hawk and Central City. The road was soon washed away in a cloudburst. Other roadbuilders tried, but storms destroyed their efforts five times, and in 1885 the route was abandoned. Bear Canyon and Bear Peak were purchased by the city between 1912 and 1917.

Connections

Bear Peak is separated from South Boulder Peak by a saddle, so both can be climbed in a single outing if you've got the energy. Just below the summit of Bear Peak on the northwest side, a trail sign marks the route to **South Boulder Peak** and to **Shadow Canyon,** which descends to the Mesa Trail (see page 106).

At the trail junction sign for Bear Canyon, Bear Peak West Ridge, and Green Bear, you can take the **Green Bear** fork up to the **Green Mountain West Ridge Trail** and to **Green Mountain** (see page 83). If you park one car at NCAR and another at the Green Mountain West Ridge Trailhead, you can make a one-way hike by connecting these trails with Bear Canyon.

Access

Park at NCAR at the very west end of Table Mesa Drive. Any access point to the Mesa Trail will also work but will be a longer hike.

South Boulder Peak via Shadow Canyon

Distance: 2.5 miles one way
Elevation: 5,600 to 8,549 feet
Highlights: Views of peaks and plains, shady coniferous forest
Difficulty: Strenuous
Topo map: Eldorado Springs

Description

Although this peak is slightly higher than Bear Peak, its profile is less familiar because it lies farther west and is hidden by Bear Peak from most vantage points. However, the views from the top are equally spectacular, and the trail up Shadow Canyon offers unique perspectives of Devils Thumb and Devils Thumb Ridge.

From the South Trailhead, follow the Mesa Trail until it enters the ponderosa pines, where the trail splits. Take the left branch past the McGillivary Cabin, now almost hidden by European poplars and overgrown shrubs. Beyond this cabin where the Mesa Trail veers north, turn left (south) and continue on the old service road that curves up to the Stockton cabin. The springs and a small pool above this cabin are good for bird and animal watching, and in early October the sumac turns a vivid red.

Just beyond the Stockton Cabin is another signpost. A right turn leads back to the Mesa Trail and is an alternative return route. A left turn leads into Shadow Canyon, a narrow, fern-filled canyon where flammulated owls and raptors nest. From here, the trail climbs very steeply, gaining about 1,620 feet in elevation in about a mile, frequently ascending via stone "stairs" past huge red boulders.

When the trail reaches the saddle between Bear Peak and South Boulder Peak, turn left (southwest) at the signpost and continue climbing. A bit of easy rock scrambling brings you to the summit where the views stretch from Longs Peak to Pikes Peak. Gross Reservoir and Walker Ranch lie below, and the plains, dotted with innumerable lakes, seem to fade into infinity to the east. You can enjoy raspberries that ripen near the summit in autumn, but leave some for the bears!

History

In October, 1920, six members of the Boulder Colorado Mountain Club stumbled upon this canyon and wrote about it in the Club's magazine, *Trail & Timberline:* "Shadow Canyon—as we are trying to name it, since it has no other name that we can discover—is a very deep, long canyon cutting in between Bear Mountain and South Boulder Peak....It is rimmed with huge, upstanding rocks 'about and all around,' whose great shadows are cast almost any time of day upon the opposite mountainside....We found it heavily wooded with spruce, cedar and pine and full of beautiful kinnikinnick patches."

The Stockton Cabin at the mouth of the canyon was probably built in the 1890s as a miner's shack. West of the cabin a mining tunnel goes into the hillside for about twelve feet, and there is another tunnel north of the cabin. Roscoe Stockton, a teacher, historian, and writer, bought the land and cabin in 1910, and his family held it until it was purchased by the city.

The McGillivary (sometimes spelled "McGilvery") Cabin is a little lower than the Stockton Cabin, near the point where the Mesa Trail turns

South Boulder Peak via Shadow Canyon

View of Devils Thumb from Shadow Canyon

north. This typical homestead cabin was probably built from handhewn logs by Seth Prudens in the 1870s, and was sold to Hugh McGillivary in 1906. The gingerbread was probably added around 1917. The outhouse, which is almost impossible to find now, was noted for its large, south-facing windows. It was hauled up from the plains where it had served as a child's playhouse.

Access
Park at the Mesa Trail South Trailhead on Eldorado Springs Drive, 2 miles west of SR 93.

Doudy Draw to Flatirons Vista

Distance: 3.3 miles one way
Elevation: 5,680 to 6,220 feet (on ridge), and down to 5,900 feet
Highlights: Views of foothills and Flatirons, wildflowers, birds, variety of habitats from riparian to grassland to pine forest
Difficulty: Easy to moderate
Topo map: Eldorado Springs, Louisville

Description
Starting at the Doudy Draw Trailhead, this trail follows a small creek and passes through stands of wild plum, hackberry, and hawthorn—wonderful habitat for brush-loving birds such as lazuli buntings, towhees, tanagers, grosbeaks, and orioles in the spring. The first 0.3 mile is paved and wheelchair-accessible, ending in a cottonwood grove picnic area. Beyond the picnic area, you cross Community Ditch and continue up the draw to the southwest. At about 1.5 miles, the trail climbs the ridge to the east, makes a large switchback halfway up, and flattens out on top of the mesa in an open ponderosa pine forest. Continue east across the grassy plateau to the Flatirons Vista Trailhead.

If you turn and look west, the views of the foothills and rock formations are spectacular, and there are occasional peeks at snowcapped peaks framed by the Eldorado Springs "gateway rocks." By leaving a car at both trailheads, you can make this a one-way hike in either direction. For exercise, start at Doudy Draw; for an easy downhill walk, start at Flatirons Vista.

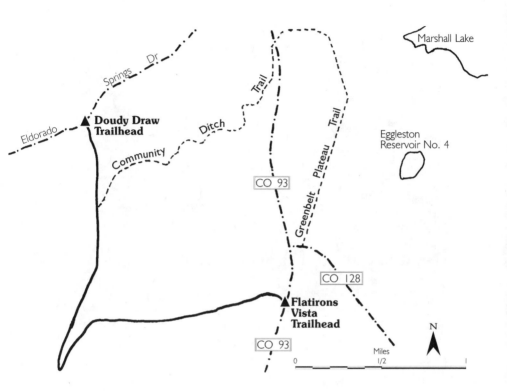

Doudy Draw to Flatirons Vista

History

Several spellings (including Douty and Dowdy) exist for the first settler in this area, but the most commonly accepted version is *Doudy*. Andrew Doudy and his son, Sylvester, ranched here during the 1850s and 1860s. Andrew also built the flour mill on Boulder Creek near present-day Settlers Park. Later, the mill was acquired by E. B. Yount, whose flour was regarded as "legal tender."

In 1993, upper Doudy Draw narrowly escaped becoming the site for two hydroelectric dams. An alert reader of the *Federal Register* noticed that a California company had applied for a permit to build two dams on City of Boulder Open Space. (A 1920s law allows companies to apply for a hydroelectric dam-building permit without having to notify the landowner, and to condemn private land for such dams.) The city found out about the proposal in time to oppose the project successfully.

Vista from Doudy Draw Trail

Connections

For a 6-mile loop hike, connect the two ends of Doudy Draw Trail with the **Greenbelt Plateau Trail** and **Community Ditch** (see page 40). There are also several unmarked trails that fork to the right of the main Doudy Draw Trail.

Access

Park at either the Flatirons Vista Trailhead on the west side of SR 93, just south of SR 128, or at the Doudy Draw Trailhead about 2 miles west of SR 93 on Eldorado Springs Drive.

South Boulder Creek Loop or Walker Ranch Loop

Distance: 7.9 miles round-trip
Elevation: 7,200 feet, with a total elevation gain of over 1000 feet via several ups and downs

Highlights: Variety of habitats from tumultuous creek to meadows to forests, wildflowers, birds, historic buildings, regeneration after fire
Difficulty: Strenuous
Topo map: Eldorado Springs

Description

Several trails and old ranch roads can be combined for an up-and-down loop variously called Walker Ranch or South Boulder Creek Loop. From the South Boulder Creek Trailhead, descend on an old road to South Boulder Creek, with views of Langridge Dyke and Castle Rock on your right. At the creek, turn right and follow it upstream to a bridge. Immediately after crossing the bridge, the trail forks. The right fork continues along the creek for a short distance and dead-ends at private property.

Take the left fork, which climbs rather steeply to Crescent Meadows and has outstanding views of the snowcapped Front Range. Turn left onto the Crescent Meadows Trail, where you enter the upper end of Eldorado Canyon State Park. The original hiking trail followed an old road to the left. The new section, built in 1994, heads down to the right and offers good views across the meadow to the ruins of several old barns, built by Carl Daniels. (Daniels married Leta Walker, James Walker's first grandchild.)

Just before South Boulder Creek, the trail descends very steeply. Severe erosion makes this section hazardous, so be careful. After crossing the creek, the trail connects with the Eldorado Canyon Trail. At this intersection a spur trail leads to the Ethel Harold Picnic Area and another parking lot. Take the left branch, which climbs to the Columbine Gulch Trail. Turn left onto the Columbine Gulch Trail, which completes the loop in another 1.25 miles.

In September 2000, a wildfire burned more than 1,000 acres on Walker Ranch and adjacent areas. It took 5 days, 500 firefighters, and $1.5 million to bring it under control. As you hike the trail, be careful of unstable areas and of dead trees and observe the rebirth of the forest. Wildflowers should be especially spectacular for a few years after the burn.

Because this trail is a favorite for mountain bikers and is crowded on weekends, it is best hiked on weekdays.

History

James and Phoebe Walker ran the largest cattle ranch on the Front Range in the late nineteenth and early twentieth centuries. James first came to the area in 1869 and lived briefly in a cabin used for miners' supplies. The original ranch house, built in 1883, burned down in 1992, but most

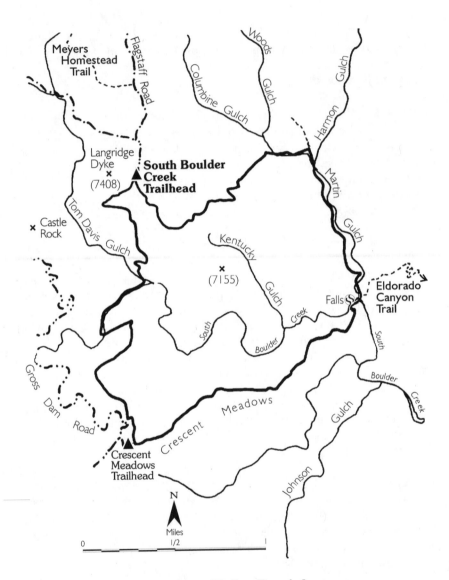

South Boulder Creek Loop or Walker Ranch Loop

Walker Ranch

of the outbuildings are still intact. However, they are closed to the public except on designated "Living History Days" when volunteers show what daily life was like in the late 1800s. The homestead, which survived the wildfire of 2000, is on the *National Register of Historic Places.*

Before the arrival of the Walkers, the Arapaho frequently camped and hunted on the land.

Connections

Other trails that originate near Walker Ranch include the **Eldorado Canyon Trail,** which goes over several ridges to Eldorado Canyon State Park in 4.4 miles, and the **Meyers Homestead Trail** (see page 116), which starts across the road from Walker Ranch.

Access

At Realization Point, 3.4 miles up Flagstaff Road, turn left and drive 4.5 miles to the South Boulder Creek Trailhead on the east side of the road. You can also start at the Crescent Meadows Trailhead on the east side of the Gross Dam Road (Flagstaff Road becomes Gross Dam Road at the dam).

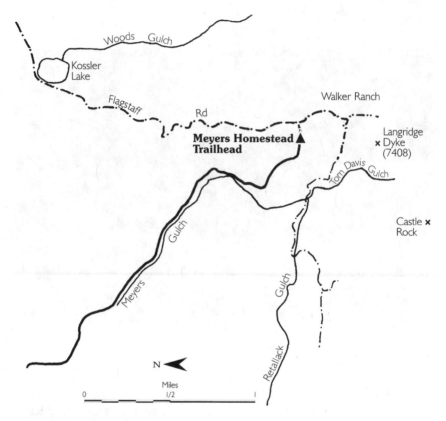

Meyers Homestead Trail

Meyers Homestead Trail

Distance: 2.5 miles one way
Elevation: 7,200 to 7,880 feet
Highlights: Wildflowers, wildlife, woodlands, scenic overlook, ruins of historic barns
Difficulty: Easy to moderate
Topo map: Eldorado Springs

Description

Starting at the picnic area a short distance northwest of Walker Ranch, an old road (closed to motorized vehicles) drops down to a meadow containing the ruins of one of James Walker's old barns. From the meadow, take the road that heads west, following a small stream (the road that goes to the barn dead-ends at private property in about 0.3 mile). Near the top,

A barn on Meyers Homestead Trail

the road veers away from the stream and curves around an upper meadow to an overlook with views of the Indian Peaks and Boulder Canyon. There are several aspen groves and flower-filled meadows along the way. In spring, bluebirds seem to sing from every fencepost, and in autumn elk may bugle.

History

Andrew R. Meyers patented this homestead in 1890 and logged most of the trees, using portable sawmills, before selling the land to James Walker. Walker was more successful than most cattlemen of his time, as he fenced the cattle, fed them in winter, and used a hardy Scottish breed. Some of the ruins of his seventeen hay barns can still be seen from the Meyers Homestead Trail.

Connections

If you cross Flagstaff Road, you can connect with several of the trails at **Walker Ranch** (see page 112).

Access

At Realization Point, 3.4 miles up Flagstaff Road, turn left and drive 4.4 miles to the Meyers Homestead Trailhead on the west side of the road.

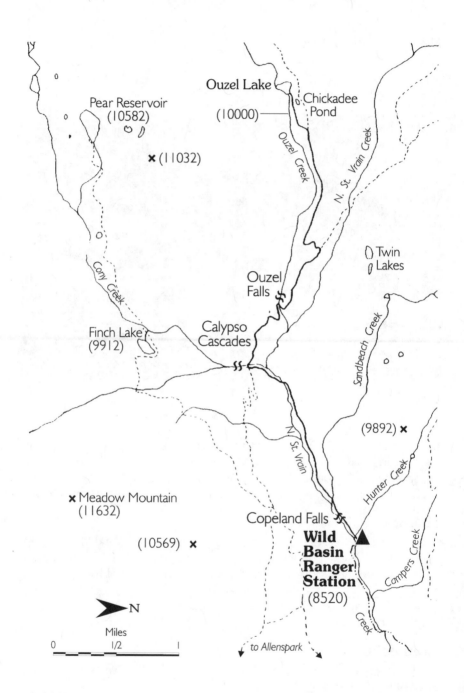

Pear Reservoir
(10582)

Ouzel Lake

(10000)

Chickadee
Pond

✗ (11032)

Ouzel Creek

N. St. Vrain Creek

○ Twin
⟩ Lakes

Ouzel
Falls

Cony Creek

Finch Lake
(9912)

Calypso
Cascades

Sandbeach Creek

○ ○

(9892) ✗

N. St. Vrain

Hunter Creek

✗ Meadow Mountain
(11632)

(10569) ✗

Copeland Falls

Wild
Basin
Ranger
Station
(8520)

Campers Creek

➤ N

Miles

0   1/2   1

to Allenspark

Creek

Wild Basin Area

Mountains

At higher elevations the foothills turn to mountains, the reason why many of us are addicted to hiking. Ecosystems include aspen woodlands, lodgepole pine forests, spruce/fir forests, mountain meadows and wetlands, and the tundra. Most of these trails are on U.S. Forest Service land and are maintained by the Forest Service. They are best hiked in summer and early fall as snow usually does not melt until late June or July and may cover the trails again by October. In winter, many of the trails (and access roads) are superb for ski touring.

Most of the trails described here are strenuous if you hike the entire distance. However, the first segments are often easy to moderate, so check the topo maps and hike only as far as is fun. Here are a few especially beautiful, but easy, sections of longer trails:

Easy
- Copeland Falls (see page 120)
- Mitchell Lake (see page 142)
- Long Lake, Jean Lunning Trail (see page 143)
- Hessie Falls (see page 168)

Easy to Moderate
- Isabelle Lake (see page 143)
- Fourth of July Mine (see page 161)

Moderate
- Calypso Cascade, Ouzel Falls (see page 120)
- Timberline Falls (see page 123)
- South St. Vrain Trail to Baptist Camp Road (see page 133)

WILD BASIN AREA

Wild Basin, in the southeastern corner of Rocky Mountain National Park (RMNP), lies in Boulder County. You'll find numerous lakes, waterfalls, peaks, and many miles of trails in the Wild Basin area, all of which are covered extensively in several books and RMNP brochures. We have limited coverage in this guide to just one trail—our favorite. But we encourage you to pick up a park brochure and explore others.

Ouzel Lake via Calypso Cascade and Ouzel Falls

(See map on page 118)

Distance: 4.9 miles one way
Elevation: 8,520 to 10,000 feet
Highlights: Waterfalls, lakes, cascading creek, wildflowers, coniferous forests, snowcapped mountain views
Difficulty: Strenuous
Topo map: Allens Park, Isolation Peak

Description

This is one of the best waterfall trails in Colorado and is a popular ski tour in the winter. For most of its length, it follows North St. Vrain Creek (so wild it looks like one continuous waterfall) through shady coniferous forests mixed with aspen. Near the end, it rewards hikers with a high mountain lake surrounded by jagged peaks. Of course, you don't have to hike the whole distance; any of the waterfalls are delightful destinations in their own right.

Rocky Mountain National Park trails are exceptionally well-maintained, providing signs giving mileage at every junction and bridges across every creek. The trail to Ouzel Lake and the connecting trails next mentioned start at the south end of the Wild Basin Ranger Station parking lot. Your first stop should be at upper and lower Copeland Falls. A side trail makes a short detour to them, whetting your appetite for the even wilder falls to come. Just beyond the falls, a rock garden on the right is filled with wildflowers in spring and summer. The main trail climbs 1.8 miles to Calypso Cascade, named for the fairy slipper orchids (*Calypso bulbosa*) that are abundant along the trail in late May and early June. At Calypso Cascade, the trail to **Finch Lake** and **Pear Lake** veers to the left. Take the Ouzel Lake Trail to the right.

At 2.7 miles, Ouzel Falls thunders on your left. There are good views from the bridge, but it's worthwhile taking the muddy side trail a short

Calypso Cascade

distance for full frontal views of this forty-foot fall, named for the water ouzels or dippers that often nest here.

From the bridge, the trail skirts a cliff and climbs to another junction, with the right fork heading to **Thunder Lake** and **Boulder-Grand Pass** and the left fork continuing on to Ouzel Lake. The Ouzel Lake trail goes up a ridge that was swept by the 1978 Allenspark forest fire. Small shrubs, a few aspen and pine, and extensive blueberry patches are revegetating the burned area, and snags of the incinerated forest still stand. One mixed blessing of the fire is that it opened up spectacular views of Longs Peak and Mount Meeker on the right, Copeland on the left, and jagged peaks in between.

The trail continues along the ridge to another junction, where the right fork goes to **Bluebird Lake** and the left fork drops slightly for half a mile to Ouzel Creek and the outlet for Ouzel Lake. There are actually *two* lakes at the end of the Ouzel Lake trail, but Chickadee Pond, hidden by a lateral moraine, is easy to miss unless you walk to the burned-over moraine behind the outhouse at the Ouzel Lake campsite.

History

Botanist William S. Cooper named many Wild Basin features, such as Calypso Cascade, when he mapped the area in 1911. This first map sold for fifteen cents. Rocky Mountain National Park was established in 1915, thanks largely to the campaign mounted by Enos Mills, a Rocky Mountain writer, naturalist, and climber who made 297 ascents of Longs Peak, and whose cabin still stands several miles beyond the Wild Basin turnoff. Enda Mills Kiley, Enos Mills's daughter, still lives near the cabin and keeps it open to the public during the summer.

The forest fire, which destroyed one thousand acres in Wild Basin, was started by lightning on August 9, 1978. The fire smoldered until September, when winds fanned the flames, threatening the town of Allenspark. A massive fire fighting effort began, and the fire was finally contained one month later.

Connections

The following trails also originate at the Wild Basin Trailhead: **Bluebird Lake** (6.3 miles), **Thunder Lake** (6.8 miles), **Finch Lake** (5.3 miles), and **Pear Lake** (7.3 miles). Near Copeland Lake, at the turnoff for Wild Basin, there is also a trailhead for **Sandbeach Lake.** All of these trails are shown on the RMNP brochure.

Access

From Boulder, take US 36 north to Lyons. Turn left onto SR 7 and continue to the Wild Basin turnoff, about 2 miles northwest of Allenspark. Turn west, drive past Wild Basin Lodge, and turn right onto a dirt road that dead-ends in 2.3 miles at the Wild Basin Ranger Station parking lot. The lot fills up during the summer, so plan to arrive early. In winter the road is usually closed about 2 miles before the ranger station.

ST. VRAIN AREA

Gibraltar Lake, St. Vrain Glaciers

(See map on pages 124–125)

Distance: 8.4 miles one way
Elevation: 8,638 to 11,200 feet
Highlights: Glaciers, alpine lakes, cascading creek, wildflowers, views of Elk Tooth Mountain, craggy ridges
Difficulty: Strenuous
Topo map: Allenspark, Isolation Peak

Description

The St. Vrain Glaciers and the topography created by them form some of the wildest, most beautiful scenery in the Indian Peaks Wilderness. It's a place of splendor. Because of its length, we recommend this trip as an overnight backpack outing rather than as a day hike. Better yet, set up a base camp for a day or two, giving yourself a chance to explore and savor the scenery and solitude.

Starting at the parking area west of Camp Dick, walk for a short distance along the road to the Buchanan Pass Trail sign. You will deposit your wilderness permit in the box here if you are backpacking. (Note: This trail was formerly called the "Middle St. Vrain Trail," and some signs still show this name.) Drop down to cross Middle St. Vrain Creek on the bridge. The Buchanan Pass Trail, closed to motorized vehicles, climbs gently through a mixed conifer and aspen forest, paralleling the north side of the creek for about 2 miles to Timberline Falls. Because the trail is used in winter for ski touring and snowshoeing, it is marked with blue diamonds.

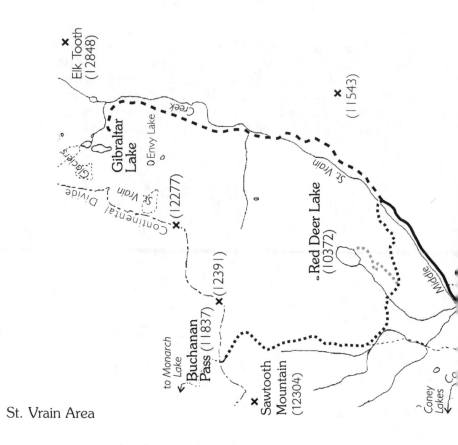

St. Vrain Area

If you have a rugged 4-wheel-drive vehicle with high clearance, you can drive the extremely rough road, FS 114, which parallels the south side of the creek for about 3.5 miles and ends across a bridge from the trail, near the Indian Peaks Wilderness boundary.

About 0.5 mile beyond the first sign for the Indian Peaks Wilderness, you'll find good campsites in a flower-filled meadow. When we were last there, the meadow was inhabited by many ground squirrels and a long-tailed weasel. At the upper edge of the meadow, the **St. Vrain Mountain Trail** branches to the right.

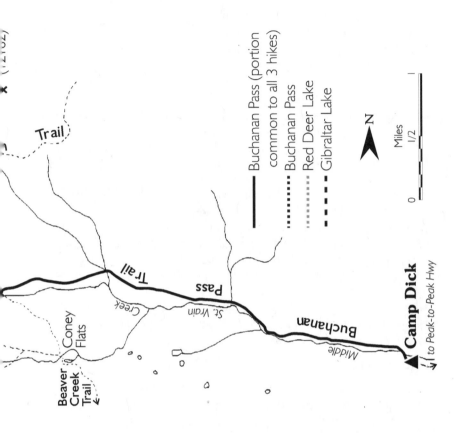

Continue straight ahead on the Buchanan Pass Trail for about 1 mile to a forest of still-standing dead trees and another meadow, which also has good campsites. At the upper end of this meadow, a trail junction sign points to the left for **Red Deer Lake** and **Buchanan Pass.** Continue up the St. Vrain Glacier Trail with a jagged, gray rock ridge to your right, the creek to your left, and Elk Tooth Mountain (elev. 12,848 feet) dominating the end of the valley. A variety of wildflowers is reclaiming the old corduroy road, and at higher elevations glacier lilies turn the slopes a buttery yellow at the edge of melting snowfields in late spring and early summer.

This old logging road narrows to a footpath that leads to the first creek crossing. Descend to the creek and, carefully, traverse the rickety logs. A stout pole is useful. Another footpath leads back to the logging road, which continues up the valley and crosses the creek again. This crossing is spanned by a solid fallen tree, scored to give better footing. An alternate route to this pair of creek crossings involves a fair amount of talus-hopping and bushwhacking. We have tried both routes, and recommend crossing the creek.

Shortly beyond the second creek crossing there is a lovely, shallow lake dotted with wooded islands. This lake, not on the maps, seems almost enchanted. Perhaps, like *Brigadoon,* it will not be there when we go again. The trail crosses a logjam at the lower end of this lake, then climbs fairly steeply, crossing several small streams, to emerge at an alpine meadow above an unnamed lake we call "Lower Gibraltar." A massive cairn at this point is a good spot to stop to enjoy the view of Elk Tooth, and to take your bearings, as the official trail seems to end here.

A short climb up either side of a braided creek brings you to Lake Gibraltar, which is shaped like a dumbbell with a small rocky rib separating the two halves. Two of the St. Vrain Glaciers plunge into the lake. Above the lake, a waterfall springs suddenly from the scree slope, falls for about ten feet, and is absorbed again by the scree.

Climb the gentle ridge southeast of the lake for wonderful views of Lake Envy below as well as views of Elk Tooth and the basin containing the Gibraltar Lakes and the St. Vrain Glaciers.

History

Logging was extensive here prior to the 1930s, especially in the area where the Buchanan Pass and the St. Vrain Glacier Trails diverge. Some stumps measure more than three feet across, and you can find traces of old cabins, bed frames and springs, bits of old machinery, and even solidified cement bags still bearing the imprint of the wrapping material.

Connections

If you are base camping, you can make day hikes on the following connecting trails: **Red Deer Lake** (see page 127), **St. Vrain Mountain** (see page 131), and **Buchanan Pass** and **Sawtooth Mountain** (see page 128). You can also make an even longer backpacking trip by continuing over Buchanan Pass to **Monarch Lake** or by connecting with the **Beaver Creek Trail** to the **Mitchell Lake** parking area.

Access

Turn west off Peak-to-Peak Highway (SR 72) at Peaceful Valley onto FS Road 114. Park just beyond the west end of the Camp Dick Campground.

Red Deer Lake via Buchanan Pass Trail

(See map on pages 124–125)

Distance: 6.9 miles one way
Elevation: 8,638 to 10,372 feet
Highlights: Timberline lake, cascading creek, wildflowers, views
Difficulty: Strenuous
Topo map: Allens Park, Isolation Peak

Description

Red Deer Lake, set in a rocky bowl under jagged cliffs, is surrounded by wind-flagged conifers, aspen, and wildflowers and is fed by snowfields and a small waterfall. The terrain is rough and rocky, but a few camping sites can be found in the trees.

Starting at the parking area west of Camp Dick, walk for a short distance along the road to the Buchanan Pass Trail sign. Follow this trail to the junction with the **St. Vrain Glacier Trail** (see page 123 for details of this first stretch).

Red Deer Lake

At the junction, turn left and cross the bridge over the Middle St. Vrain Creek, and contour for about 1 mile. Turn right onto Red Deer Lake Trail. A short, steep climb brings you to Red Deer Lake.

Several old roads and trails, now out of service, are shown on the USGS topo maps. However, the main trail is obvious and well-marked.

History

Immediately after crossing Middle St. Vrain Creek you can see many slab piles from sawmills that were active prior to 1930.

Connections

From Red Deer Lake you can drop back to the **Buchanan Pass Trail** and continue up to the pass and **Sawtooth Mountain** (see next trail description). This trail also connects to **Beaver Creek Trail,** which goes to the Mitchell Lake parking area, with other junctions to **Mount Audubon** (see page 139) and to **Coney Lake.** Or, you can return to the **St. Vrain Glacier Trail** and climb to Gibraltar Lake and the St. Vrain Glaciers (see page 123).

Access

From the Peak-to-Peak Highway (SR 72), turn west at Peaceful Valley onto FS Road 114. Park just beyond the west side of the Camp Dick Campground.

Buchanan Pass and Sawtooth Mountain via the Buchanan Pass Trail

(See map on pages 124–125)

Distance: 9.5 miles one way
Elevation: 8,638 to 11,837 feet at Buchanan Pass, and 12,304 feet at Sawtooth Mountain
Highlights: Spectacular views, alpine wildflowers and wildlife
Difficulty: Strenuous
Topo map: Allens Park, Isolation Peak

Description

Sawtooth Mountain looks like a giant, snaggled tooth rising from the rolling tundra and is the extreme eastern point of the Continental Divide in the United States. It dominates the skyline for many miles, and is easier to

Sawtooth Mountain, as seen from the Sourdough Trail

climb than it appears. However, a long hike with considerable elevation gain is necessary before actually starting the summit climb, so backpacking into the general vicinity makes for an easier trip.

Starting at the parking area west of Camp Dick, walk for a short distance along the road to the Buchanan Pass Trail sign and follow this trail to the junction with the **St. Vrain Glacier Trail** (see page 123 for details on this first stretch).

At the junction, turn left toward Middle St. Vrain Creek. Go across the bridge and contour for about 1 mile to another trail junction, where the **Red Deer Lake Trail** leads uphill to the right. Continue on the **Buchanan Pass Trail,** which continues straight ahead, contouring around the ridge to the Beaver Creek Trail junction. Turn right and head up the valley over several easy stream crossings, with the main creek staying to your left. As the subalpine habitat shifts to krummholz and tundra, look for the low point on the ridge ahead. That's Buchanan Pass.

The trail zigzags around the left side of a small buttress into a small alpine meadow and crosses to the other side of the basin, where it makes a switchback and then continues on up to the pass. Large snowfields persist until late in the season and may conceal parts of the trail. In heavy snow years, these snowfields can last through the entire summer.

From the pass, turn left (southeast) and climb the ridge 0.4 mile to the summit of Sawtooth. No technical skills are needed, and the route is obvious.

History

Archaeologist Jim Benedict has identified many hunting blinds and low stone walls used by prehistoric people for communal game drives on the tundra near Buchanan Pass. Like most game drives above treeline, these walls make a rough, upside-down V to funnel the animals uphill and downwind toward the narrow end, where most of the blinds were built. Benedict also directed the excavation of a hunting camp and butchering stations below Coney Lake. Some stone points date to approximately 5,700 years ago. Bighorn sheep, formerly plentiful here, have been reintroduced into the North St. Vrain Creek drainage and are spreading back into this area.

The pass, probably named for President Buchanan who signed the bill that created the Colorado Territory in 1861, was used as a stage road in the early 1890s. Over the years, various roads and railroads were planned for this route, and as recently as 1967 a toll road and tunnel were proposed.

Connections

If you are base camping, you can make day hikes to **Red Deer Lake** (see page 127) and to **Gibraltar Lake** and the **St. Vrain Glaciers** (see page 123). You can also make a longer backpacking trip by continuing over Buchanan Pass to **Monarch Lake** or by connecting with the **Beaver Creek Trail** to the Mitchell Lake parking area, with other junctions to **Mount Audubon** (see page 139) and to **Coney Lake.**

Access

From the Peak-to-Peak Highway (SR 72), turn west at Peaceful Valley onto FS Road 114. Park just beyond the west side of the Camp Dick Campground.

An alternative route for reaching Buchanan Pass and Sawtooth Mountain is to turn west onto CR 96 from the Peak-to-Peak Highway (SR 72) and continue to Coney Flats Road at the northwest end of Beaver Reservoir, just beyond the spillway. From Coney Flats, you can easily hike the Beaver Creek Trail to its junction with the Buchanan Pass Trail. However, the Coney Flats Road (high clearance, 4-wheel drive only) is so bad that it's almost easier to hike it than it is to jeep it.

St. Vrain Mountain

Distance: 4.5 miles one way
Elevation: 8,900 to 12,162 feet
Highlights: Aspen to alpine habitats, wildflowers, views of Longs Peak, Wild Basin, the Indian Peaks, and the plains
Difficulty: Strenuous
Topo map: Allens Park

Description

Starting in a forest of lodgepole pine and aspen, the St. Vrain Mountain Trail reaches the Indian Peaks Wilderness boundary in about 0.5 mile. Soon after, it comes to a branch of Rock Creek that it parallels up through a more open hillside to an old burn area, where it zigzags away from the creek. Eventually, the trail returns to and crosses the creek, and climbs the opposite hillside through a mixed conifer forest to an alpine saddle between Meadow Mountain to the east and St. Vrain Mountain to the west.

At the Rocky Mountain National Park boundary sign, the trail swings south across the tundra, offering great views of Longs Peak, the surrounding mountains, and Wild Basin. The easiest route to the summit of St. Vrain Mountain starts at the saddle on the east flank of the mountain. There is no official trail to the top, but it's not difficult to see the route that climbs about 700 additional feet, partly across talus, to the summit. Beyond the saddle, the St. Vrain Mountain Trail continues for 3 miles to the Buchanan Pass Trail.

For hikers not interested in peak-bagging, the trail up to the alpine saddle between St. Vrain and Meadow Mountains (about 3 miles and 2,400 feet of elevation gain) is well worthwhile—especially in late June and early July when the tundra is in bloom. This part of the trail goes up a south-facing bowl that gets very warm and is good for early flowers. Deep snowdrifts may persist in the spruce/fir forest below the saddle, even as flowers bloom above and below them. In mid-August, mushrooms are usually plentiful along the lower portion of the trail, and in late September the aspen turn to gold. The lower section, including the unplowed part of Ski Road, is also good for ski touring in winter.

History

According to some stories, the Rock Creek Ski Area predated World War II and was operated with a single rope tow.

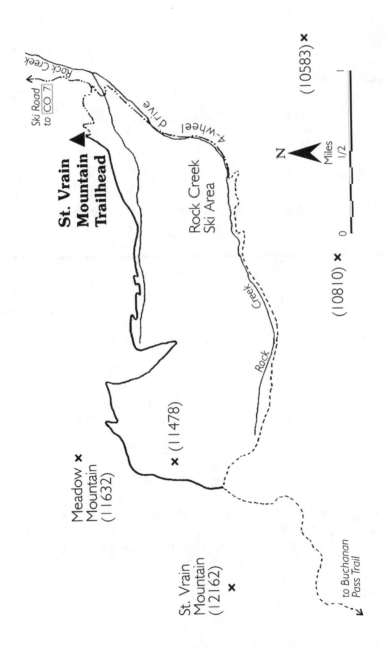

St. Vrain Mountain

Connections

Although there is no official trail up **Meadow Mountain** (elev. 11,632 feet), the route is obvious from the saddle and the final ascent is quite easy. At the RMNP boundary sign, turn right and climb until you're there.

The St. Vrain Mountain Trail intersects two other trails, **Buchanan Pass** (see page 128) and **Rock Creek,** either of which can be combined for long loops. The Rock Creek Trail begins where Ski Road dead-ends and is an alternate route (about 1 mile) for climbing St. Vrain Mountain. However, the trail is difficult to find and is not maintained by the Forest Service.

Access

From Boulder, take US 36 north to Lyons. Turn left onto SR 7 and continue to Ferncliff. Turn left onto old SR 7 (now the business loop between Ferncliff and Allenspark). Follow the old highway to Ski Road (CR 107), just east of Allenspark. Turn left and continue to a fork in 1.7 miles. Take the right fork, which dead-ends in 0.5 mile at the St. Vrain Mountain Trailhead.

South St. Vrain Trail to Brainard Lake

Distance: 5 miles one way
Elevation: 8,760 to 10,440 feet
Highlights: Mixed aspen and conifer forests, wildflowers, some streamside habitat
Difficulty: Strenuous
Topo map: Ward, Gold Hill

Description

Starting at the South St. Vrain Trailhead, the trail (FS Trail 909) is well marked with signs and blue diamonds. It parallels South St. Vrain Creek through meadows and aspen groves and then leaves the creek to continue uphill through a mixed aspen and coniferous forest. At various points the trail swings back to the creek, but this first section is the best riparian area and is especially nice in late spring and early summer, and in September when the aspen turn golden.

In about 2 miles, the trail joins a dirt road leading to the Baptist Camp. For a short, easy hike, turn around at this point and retrace the route down.

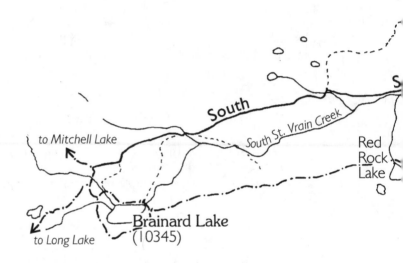

South St. Vrain Trail to Brainard Lake

To continue to Brainard Lake, walk up the road to a Forest Service sign and turn right onto a trail that bypasses private property. Continue on this trail past two signs pointing to Stapp Lakes (these trails branch off to the right). At the second Stapp Lakes sign, a third trail joins the main trail from the Baptist Camp on the left. Continue on the main trail up to a major trail intersection where the **Sourdough** and the South St. Vrain Trails join—the halfway point on the South St. Vrain route to Brainard Lake. The left fork at this intersection goes up to the Red Rock Trailhead. Stay on the main trail, which heads up to a T-junction. The right fork goes to Beaver Reservoir. Take the left fork and continue past three more junctions (the Waldrop Ski Trail enters and later exits from the left, and a third branch goes to the Brainard Lake parking area) to end at a small parking area above the Brainard Lake Road, near the

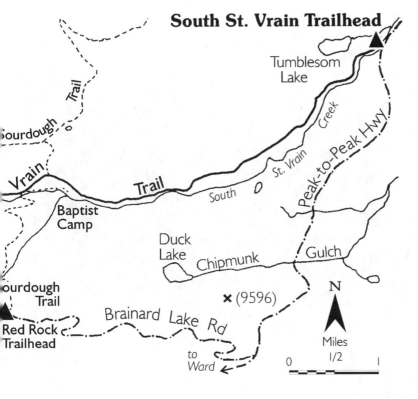

Colorado Mountain Club cabin built in 1928. It's recorded that during one 1929 CMC outing, the men, clad only in boots and skis, followed a track near the cabin and skinny-dipped in a seven-foot drift at the bottom of the hill.

Except for a narrow, icy section near the beginning, this trail is good for ski touring and snowshoeing in winter.

This is a complicated description because of the net-like Brainard Lake trail system. A map is very helpful.

History

The trail connecting Brainard Lake and the Baptist Camp follows an old logging road, one of several in the area. The land for the Baptist Camp was donated by Bertha James in 1945, and the first cabins were originally World War II Air Force barracks moved in from Buckley Field in 1949. The camp is still used today by the First Baptist Church of Boulder.

Road to Baptist Camp off of the South St. Vrain Trail

Connections

The trail lends itself to one-way hikes or ski tours if you leave one car at the Red Rock Trailhead or at Brainard Lake and another at the South St. Vrain Trailhead. You can connect with either the **Sourdough Trail** (see page 147) or the **Henry Waldrop Trail,** which begins a short distance above the Red Rock Trailhead at a gate that closes the road in winter.

You can also take either the **Baptiste** or the **Wapiti Trails** that form a loop off the Sourdough Trail, but they are only maintained for winter use.

Access

From the intersection of the Brainard Lake Road and the Peak-to-Peak Highway (SR 72), drive north 2.7 miles on the Peak-to-Peak Highway. Turn west at the sign for the Tahosa Boy Scout Camp and park along the road just west of the bridge.

Ceran St. Vrain Trail to Miller Rock

Distance: 3 miles one way
Elevation: 8,330 to 7,960 feet, and on to 8,646 feet
Highlights: Cascading creek, rock formations, wildflowers
Difficulty: Moderate
Topo map: Raymond, Gold Hill

Description

Starting at a bridge that crosses a swirling cascade, this trail follows South St. Vrain Creek 2 miles downhill to an old jeep road, losing about 400 feet. In spring, this section of the trail is almost like a rain forest path that passes through pine, Douglas-fir, spruce, and aspen trees, never losing sight or sound of the roaring creek. In late May and early June, it's one of the best places to find large clusters of fairy slipper orchids.

When the trail intersects the jeep road, turn left and follow the road uphill (away from the creek) to the top of a ridge where a side trail forks to the left. Ignore this trail, and continue on the road that drops slightly, crosses two intermittent streams, and climbs again to a small plateau in a ponderosa pine stand. At this point several old jeep roads intermingle, and it's easy to get confused. Continue on the main road past an old prospector's pit (about 10 feet to the right of the road) to a small aspen grove about 150 feet beyond the pit. At this point you can see Longs Peak through the trees, and the jeep road forks. Turn left at the fork and continue steeply uphill to another fork. The left fork drops back down to the plateau, so take the right fork, which continues uphill past a smallish rock outcropping and on to Miller Rock, a massive granitic formation with splendid views of the Indian Peaks. A faint trail circles the base of the rocks, and it's fairly easy to scramble to the top.

History

The trail is named for Ceran St. Vrain (1802–1870), a fur trader who founded several forts with his partner, Charles Bent. Fort St. Vrain, at the confluence of this creek and the South Platte River, was one of his establishments. He was also active in business, politics, and military affairs.

Connections

The assorted jeep roads you encounter along the latter part of the route can be hiked for varying distances. The middle jeep road drops down to a road that connects the towns of Raymond and Riverside, the only route

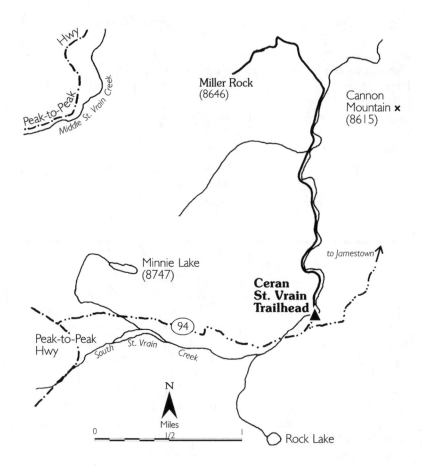

Ceran St. Vrain Trail to Miller Rock

off the mountain with a legal public access unless you return to the Ceran St. Vrain Trailhead.

Access

From Lefthand Canyon (CR 106), take CR 94 to Jamestown. From the Jamestown post office, continue another 4.7 miles to the large sign for Ceran St. Vrain. Turn right on the dirt road that dead-ends at the trailhead. The trail can also be reached from the Peak-to-Peak Highway (SR 72) by turning east on CR 94.

BRAINARD LAKE AREA

Brainard Lake is the hub for many trails leading into the Indian Peaks Wilderness and up to the tundra. The area west of Brainard Lake is managed for day use only. Permits from the Forest Service are required for overnight backpacking trips into other parts of this heavily used wilderness. The entire area is superb for wildflowers and alpine scenery. To reach Brainard Lake, take CR 102, which heads west off the Peak-to-Peak Highway just above Ward. There is a small fee during the summer to use the area beyond Red Rocks Lake. Here are some of our favorite trails originating near Brainard Lake, probably named for Colonel Wesley Brainard who prospected in the area for twenty years in the late 1800s, developing many claims.

Mount Audubon

(See map on page 140)

Distance: 3.8 miles one way
Elevation: 10,480 to 13,223 feet
Highlights: Dramatic views of peaks and plains, alpine wildflowers
Difficulty: Strenuous
Topo map: Ward

Description

This prominent mountain, which can be seen from many points in Boulder County, looks like a dish of ice cream with one spoonful taken from the side. Because it is one of the many Indian Peaks, the views from the summit are especially dramatic. Imagine looking *down* on Mount Toll! Two-thirds of the trail lies above timberline so the views and the alpine wildflowers en route are also magnificent.

Starting at the Beaver Creek Trailhead on the north side of the Mitchell Lake parking area, climb gently through coniferous forest and krummholz to emerge above timberline in 1.5 miles at a junction. The Beaver Creek Trail continues another 3.7 miles to Coney Flats. Take the left fork, which climbs steeply for another 2 miles to the summit of Mount Audubon. Cairns mark the trail above timberline and are very helpful when snowfields cover parts of the trail early in the season. The final scramble to the top involves some talus, but the route is well marked by cairns. The summit is flat and fairly

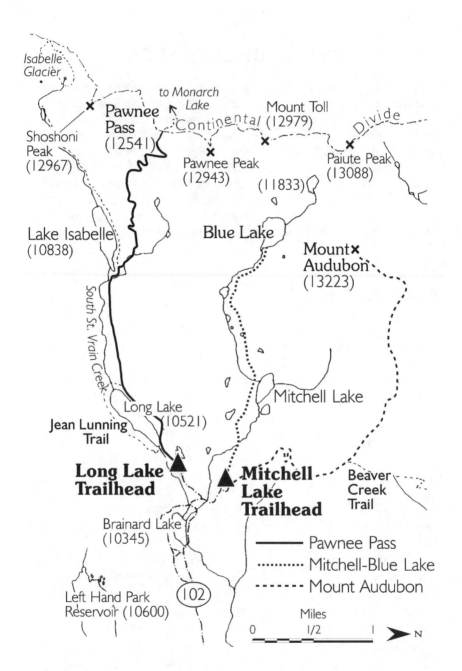

Isabelle
Glacier

Pawnee
Pass
(12541)

to Monarch Lake

Continental

Mount Toll
(12979)

Divide

Shoshoni
Peak
(12967)

Pawnee Peak
(12943)

(11833)

Paiute Peak
(13088)

Lake Isabelle
(10838)

Blue Lake

Mount×
Audubon
(13223)

South St. Vrain Creek

Long Lake
(10521)

Mitchell Lake

Jean Lunning
Trail

**Long Lake
Trailhead**

**Mitchell
Lake
Trailhead**

Beaver
Creek
Trail

Brainard Lake
(10345)

Left Hand Park
Reservoir (10600)

(102)

———— Pawnee Pass

·········· Mitchell-Blue Lake

------- Mount Audubon

Miles

0   1/2   1   ➤ N

Brainard Lake Area

The magnificent Indian Peaks, as seen from the summit of Mount Audubon

large with several waist-high stone windbreaks. This is one of the easier 13,000-foot peaks to climb, and the rewards are well worth the effort. Plan to get to the top before noon to avoid afternoon thunderstorms.

History

Botanist C. C. Parry and zoologist J. W. Velie climbed the mountain in 1864 and named it for the famous naturalist and painter, who never visited Colorado.

In 1914, Ellsworth Bethel drew a sketch map of the Indian Peaks for the U.S. Board of Geographic Names. He suggested naming the peaks for Western American Indian tribes. Eleven of his proposed names were accepted, including Apache, Arikaree, Navajo, Ogalalla, Pawnee, Paiute, and Shoshone.

Connections

At the junction of the Mount Audubon and Beaver Creek Trails, you can take the right fork for another 3.7 miles to **Coney Flats.** From Coney Flats you can climb another 1.7 miles to the **Buchanan Pass Trail** (see page 128). From the Mitchell Lake parking area, another trail leads to **Mitchell** and **Blue Lakes** (see next trail description).

Access

Take CR 102 west from the Peak-to-Peak Highway (SR 72). At the end of CR 102, circle Brainard Lake to the junction for the Long and the Mitchell Lake parking areas. Turn right and continue past the Long Lake turnoff to the Mitchell Lake parking area.

Blue Lake via Mitchell Lake

(See map on page 140)

Distance: 2.5 miles one way
Elevation: 10,480 to 11,320 feet
Highlights: Lakes, creeks, mountains, wildflowers, forest
Difficulty: Moderate
Topo map: Ward

Description

Blue Lake is one of the gems of the Indian Peaks Wilderness Area. Mount Toll (elev. 12,979 feet) rises majestically above it, a waterfall cascades into its upper end, and wildflowers surround it. Starting at the Mitchell Lake Trailhead, the well-marked trail climbs through a coniferous forest to Mitchell Lake in 1 mile. It skirts the left-hand side of the lake, crosses a creek on logs, and climbs through subalpine terrain to Blue Lake, which nestles into tussocky knolls at timberline. Parrys primrose, mertensia, and candytuft are especially luxuriant at the creek crossing just beyond Mitchell Lake, and several tarns grace the way between the two lakes. Just before the final climb to Blue Lake, a lovely, broad cascade flows from beneath a snowbank.

Connections

A steep, difficult climb from the upper end of Blue Lake, involving talus-scrambling and snowfields, leads to a saddle between **Pawnee Peak** and **Mount Toll,** and from there to either summit. Although you can see occasional signs of a trail along this route, it is not officially maintained, and the snowfield on Mount Toll can be dangerous. It's possible—but strenuous—to cross the saddle, drop down to the **Pawnee Pass Trail** (see page 143) and return to the Mitchell Lake parking area via Isabelle and Long

Hiker takes in views of Mount Toll from Blue Lake

Lakes. Note that the entire section between Blue Lake and Pawnee Pass Trail is off-trail and difficult. Take along a topo map.

The trail to **Mount Audubon** (see page 139) also begins at the Mitchell Lake parking area.

Access

Take CR 102 west from the Peak-to-Peak Highway (SR 72). At the end of CR 102, circle Brainard Lake to the junction for the Long Lake and the Mitchell Lake parking areas. Turn right and continue past the Long Lake turnoff to the Mitchell Lake parking area.

Pawnee Pass via Long Lake and Lake Isabelle

(See map on page 140)

Distance: 4.6 miles one way
Elevation: 10,520 to 12,541 feet
Highlights: Spectacular views, wildflowers, lakes, cascading creeks, tundra

Difficulty: Strenuous
Topo map: Ward

Description

Surrounded by craggy peaks and pointy gendarmes (pinnacles on a ridge), this pass is one of our favorites. However, it's not necessary to hike all the way to the pass to enjoy the trail. The quarter-mile stroll to Long Lake affords unsurpassed views across the lake to Navajo (note the "organ player" on the west side) and Apache Peaks. The 2-mile hike to Lake Isabelle is also an easy way to experience some of the best scenery in the Indian Peaks Wilderness.

Starting at the Long Lake Trailhead, the trail goes through spruce/fir forests and crosses the wilderness boundary at Long Lake. The **Jean Lunning Scenic Trail** (about a 2.5-mile loop if you circle the lake) branches to the left at the lower end of Long Lake, and the Pawnee Pass Trail skirts to the right. The Jean Lunning Scenic Trail rejoins the Pawnee Pass Trail shortly beyond the upper end of the lake. The trail to **Niwot Ridge** branches off from the Jean Lunning Trail at the upper end of the first meadow. Even if you don't take the Jean Lunning Trail, it's worth going a few steps out of your way to the outlet of Long Lake for the view.

Take the Pawnee Pass Trail on the right-hand side of Long Lake and climb gently through the forest, making a couple of switchbacks before reaching Lake Isabelle. Early in the season a broad, rippling cascade gushes out of a snowbank below this lake. Just before reaching Lake Isabelle, cross the South St. Vrain Creek on stepping stones and climb a small ridge, emerging slightly above the lake. Isabelle is an irrigation lake and is usually drained in late August. If the lake itself is your goal, check with the Forest Service to determine whether it still holds water.

At the first view of Lake Isabelle, the trail splits, with the **Isabelle Glacier Trail** leading straight ahead, skirting the right-hand side of the lake, and climbing to Isabelle Glacier in another 1.7 miles. The Pawnee Pass Trail turns to the right and crosses the creek three times before zigzagging through the last outposts of trees into fields of tundra and talus. The views looking down into Lake Isabelle, which is often tinted a jade green by glacial milk, are splendid. En route, you pass several tarns, bogs, and meadows and go through several miles of alpine flowers. Snowfields often persist until late in the season, especially the large snowfield across the trail just before the pass.

Upon reaching Pawnee Pass, it's worth descending the other side for a few switchbacks or so to see the dramatic gendarmes on the west side. If

Lake Isabelle

you continue to drop, you will reach Pawnee Lake in 2 miles, Crater Lake in 5 miles, or Monarch Lake in 11 miles. From the pass, you can climb Pawnee (elev. 12,943 feet) or Shoshone (elev. 12,967 feet) Peaks, or several other Indian Peaks. It's possible (but difficult) to make a loop trip, crossing Pawnee Peak and dropping down between Pawnee Peak and Mount Toll to Blue and Mitchell Lakes, and then back to the Long Lake trailhead. There are no marked trails to the peaks, so a topo map and backcountry experience are essential.

History

When the pass was surveyed for a railroad route in 1882, Canadian Native Americans carried in bread and other supplies over a saddle just south of Pawnee Pass, hence the trail's former name of "Breadline Trail." Pawnee Pass Trail was built during Franklin Delano Roosevelt's presidency by the Civilian Conservation Corps.

Fred Fair, Boulder City Engineer in the early 1900s, discovered Isabelle and Fair Glaciers early in the twentieth century and named Isabelle Glacier and Lake Isabelle for his wife. After he died in 1935, his ashes were scattered over the two glaciers.

Niwot Ridge, the long stretch of tundra across the Isabelle Lake drainage from Pawnee Pass, was established as one of only seventeen long-term ecological research stations in the country in 1980 by the National Science Foundation. The site is internationally famous for alpine research conducted by the University of Colorado Mountain Research Station.

Connections

The following trails connect to the Pawnee Pass Trail and are more fully described previously in this trail description: **Jean Lunning Trail, Niwot Ridge Trail,** and the **Isabelle Glacier Trail.** The **Mitchell** and **Blue Lake Trail** is described on page 142.

Access

Take CR 102 west from the Peak-to-Peak Highway (SR 72). At the end of CR 102, circle Brainard Lake to the junction for the Long and Mitchell Lake parking areas. Turn right and continue to the Long Lake turnoff (to the left) and parking area.

Sourdough Trail

Distance: About 12 miles one way. This trail is being realigned, so mileages will change in the near future.
Elevation: 8,638 feet (Camp Dick) to 9,160 feet (Beaver Reservoir) to 9,960 feet (Brainard Lake Road) to 9,200 feet (Rainbow Lakes Road)
Highlights: Good ski touring, shady coniferous forest
Difficulty: Strenuous for entire trail; moderate for individual segments
Topo map: Allens Park, Ward

Description

Three segments, described in the following paragraphs from north to south, comprise this long trail (FS 835) that stretches from Peaceful Valley to the Rainbow Lakes Road, with numerous ups and downs. Built chiefly for ski touring and mountain bicycling, the route is clearly marked by blue diamonds and arrows and stays mainly in the forest where it is protected from the worst winds. The Forest Service is still working on this trail, so be alert for changes.

It's feasible to do a two-car, one-way hike or ski trip on any of the segments or to combine the Sourdough with other trails for a variety of loops. If you're using two cars and connecting with other trails, check a topo map to determine what routes have the least elevation gain.

Camp Dick Campground to Beaver Reservoir (about 2 miles, 522-foot elevation gain). The best starting point for this segment of the Sourdough Trail is just beyond the west end of the Camp Dick Campground at a small parking area. From the parking area, walk along FS Road 921 for a short distance to where the Buchanan Pass Trail crosses the road. (Buchanan Pass Trail was formerly called "Middle St. Vrain Trail," and signs with this name may still exist.) At the trail sign on the *left* side of the road, turn left onto the Buchanan Pass Trail, which goes gently up and down past several small stream crossings and through a lush coniferous forest. At about 0.5 mile, just past a spur to Camp Dick, is the Sourdough Trail junction. Turn right and climb up to a T-junction. Twinflower (botanist Carolus Linnaeus's favorite flower and somewhat uncommon on the eastern side of the Continental Divide) grows profusely along this north-facing slope. At the T-junction, the right branch goes to the north end of Beaver Reservoir, connecting to the Coney Flats Road, while the main Sourdough Trail continues to the left. Several unmarked side trails intersect the main trail, which meanders up and down

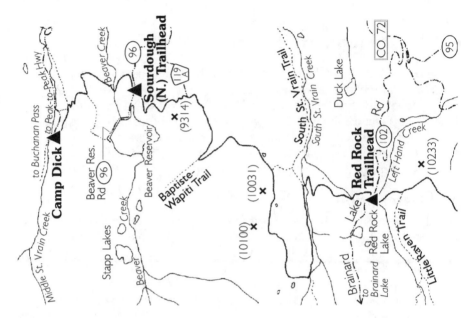

Sourdough Trail (Courtesy of Harlan Barton and the Colorado Mountain Club)

in a generally east to southeast direction and eventually crosses Beaver Creek. From the bridge, the trail contours around a small hill up to the Beaver Reservoir Road.

In winter the road into Camp Dick is not plowed, so the trail starts at the parking area where the Peak-to-Peak Highway (SR 72) crosses Middle St. Vrain Creek at Peaceful Valley, adding about a mile to the distance. There is another access point just east of the bridge at Peaceful Valley Campground. The mile-long stretch of the Buchanan Pass Trail between the two camp-grounds is a lovely walk where you'll see many blue columbines in July.

Beaver Reservoir to Brainard Lake (about 5 miles, 800-foot elevation gain). The second segment of the trail starts at the sign to your left just before you reach Beaver Reservoir, across the Beaver Reservoir Road from the previous section. The trail climbs through an area that burned in 1988. The stark, dead trees are now enveloped in a profusion of wildflowers in summer, and small aspens are thriving. When the aspens mature, this section should be a beautiful fall hike. The proliferation of trails and old roads in this vicinity can be confusing, so keep an eye out for blue diamonds.

Continue following the diamonds up through a mixed coniferous

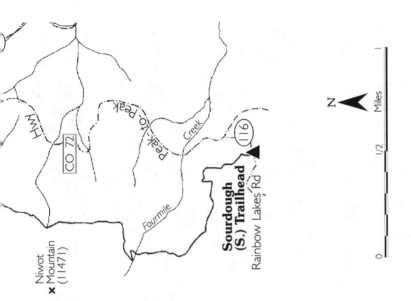

and aspen forest to a sign for the **Baptiste-Wapiti Ski Trail**, a loop maintained only for ski touring. At this point, the main trail makes a hairpin turn to the left and continues climbing until it levels out in a large meadow with views of the Indian Peaks. Twin ponds in the meadow are classic examples of the process of eutrophication: One pond is almost totally filled in with reeds, and the other (called Fresno or Dry Lake) has dried up to a fraction of its original size, as indicated by the shoreline. This stretch of the trail through aspen groves is a colorful September hike.

At frequent intervals, side trails, well marked by the Forest Service, intersect the Sourdough Trail. Several of these trails go through private property with no public access and are so marked. Just beyond Fresno Lake, the Sourdough Trail branches. This section is scheduled for realignment, so watch carefully for blue diamonds and trail markers. Follow the trail to a bridge across South St. Vrain Creek. Cross the bridge and climb up to Brainard Road below Red Rock Lake.

Brainard Road to Rainbow Lakes Road (about 5 miles, 760-foot elevation loss). The third segment starts across the road from the Red Rock Trailhead, dropping to a bridge across Left Hand Creek. At about

Some of the scenery along the Sourdough Trail, near Beaver Reservoir

0.5 mile, the **Little Raven Trail** branches to the right, while the Sourdough contours around the lower flanks of Niwot Mountain, eventually crossing the Peace Memorial Bridge over Fourmile Creek. The trail stays mostly in coniferous forest, mixed with some aspen. Occasionally, "windows" open to give views across the foothills to the plains and snowcapped peaks to the south. There are several small elevation gains and losses, but the trail generally follows the 10,000-foot contour line until near the end, where it drops rather steeply to Rainbow Lakes Road (CR 116).

History

Camp Dick was a Civilian Conservation Corps (CCC) camp in the 1930s. CCC workers built 45 miles of trails in addition to building roads, dams, and fighting fires in the Indian Peaks area. In fact, the Sourdough Trail is (partly) a collection of some of these old roads.

Connections

The main connecting trails are **Buchanan Pass Trail** (see page 128), **South St. Vrain Trail** (see page 133), and **Little Raven Trail** (see next trail description). Laterals also connect with trails that lead into the Indian Peaks Wilderness Area.

Access

All the trailheads are west of the Peak-to-Peak Highway (SR 72). The four main access points are:

• **Camp Dick Campground** on the Middle St. Vrain Road (5.8 miles north of Ward, 0.5 mile west of Peaceful Valley).
• **Beaver Creek Trailhead** on the left-hand side of CR 96 just east of Beaver Reservoir (2.5 miles north of Ward, 2 miles west on CR 96).
• **Red Rock Trailhead** on the right-hand side of CR 102 just east of Red Rock Lake (2.6 miles west on Brainard Lake Road).
• **Sourdough Trailhead** along Rainbow Lakes Road (4.7 miles south of Ward or 7 miles north of Nederland and 0.4 mile west on CR 116).

Little Raven Trail to Left Hand Reservoir

Distance: 2.5 miles one way
Elevation: 9,960 to 10,638 feet
Highlights: Views of the Indian Peaks from the Reservoir, shady coniferous forest, good ski touring
Difficulty: Moderate
Topo map: Ward

Description

Little Raven Trail, built chiefly for ski touring, branches to the right from the Sourdough Trail 0.5 mile south of the Red Rock Trailhead. It then climbs steeply to join the Left Hand Reservoir Road. It follows the road for about half a mile to a fork, where the road continues to the reservoir and the Little Raven Trail veers to the right.

In summer, the walk through the shady forest to the reservoir is pleasant, and the panoramic views across the lake to the Indian Peaks and to Longs Peak are spectacular. We recommend that you retrace this route back, or walk down the road, rather than continuing on the Little Raven Trail down to the **CMC South Trail,** which returns to Brainard Lake Road near Red Rock Lake, just above the turnoff for Lefthand Reservoir. While this combination of trails makes a wonderful ski touring loop (about 7.7

Little Raven Trail to Left Hand Reservoir

miles) in winter, it can be difficult to follow in summer because of down timber, bogs, and rock falls. In addition, the CMC South Trail is also a ditch,
often filled with water. The ditch was probably built to serve the Utica Mine
near Ward in the late 1800s. This mining company patented Brainard Lake
in 1898 and later sold it to the Forest Service. If you decide to hike the
CMC South Trail loop, watch very carefully for blue diamonds and arrows
as the trail is easy to lose and involves some bushwhacking.

History

The trail is named for Little Raven (1810–1889), Chief of the Southern Arapaho, who was forced to lead his tribe of nomadic hunters to a
sedentary life on an Oklahoma reservation after the Treaty of 1867.

Left Hand Reservoir was built by the Left Hand Ditch Company in
1966. Although it is on private land, public use of the area is permitted.
The chimneys on the CMC South Trail are from several old recreation res-
idences formerly permitted in the national forest.

Connections

In winter, the **Left Hand Park Reservoir Road** is excellent for ski
touring, but it's somewhat dull for hiking in summer. You can also go either
direction on the **Sourdough Trail** (see page 147).

Access

From the Peak-to-Peak Highway (SR 72), turn west on the Brainard Lake Road (CR 102) and continue for 2.6 miles. Park at the Red Rock Trailhead just east of Red Rock Lake. The Little Raven sign is on the left (east) side of the road.

RAINBOW LAKES AREA

Rainbow Lakes

(See map on pages 154–155)

Distance: 1 mile one way to upper lakes
Elevation: 9,920 to 10,280 feet
Highlights: Lakes, coniferous forest, wildflowers
Difficulty: Easy
Topo map: Ward

Description

The Rainbow Lakes Trail climbs gently through a mixed coniferous and aspen forest. You will also find several stands of limber pine twisted into shapes like lyres and candelabras. The trail leads to a string of small lakes containing self-sustaining populations of brook trout.

Starting at the west end of the Rainbow Lakes Campground, the trail (an old road that narrows to a trail) soon passes a wilderness boundary sign and veers to the left, away from the old road. The trail rejoins the road and reaches the first lake, partly filled with pond lilies, in about 0.5 mile, then continues on to the second lake. After the second lake, you come to a boggy area and a small creek crossing. A short climb up a rocky ridge brings you to a double lake, separated by a narrow band of rocks. The trail eventually peters out above these lakes. Return via the route you came up.

History

The road to Rainbow Lakes was completed in 1925. It was envisioned by many people to be the start of a road over Arapaho Pass to Grand Lake, with a branch to the Arapaho Glacier Overlook.

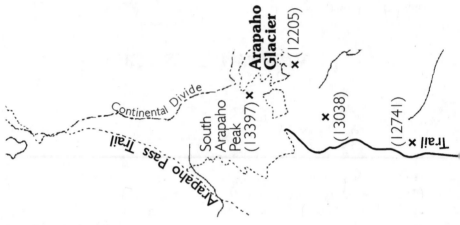

Rainbow Lakes Area

Connections

Arapaho Glacier Trail (see next trail description) also begins at the Rainbow Lakes Campground.

Access

From the Peak-to-Peak Highway (SR 72) halfway between Nederland and Ward, turn west onto CR 116 at the University of Colorado Mountain Research Station sign. This rough, gravel road dead-ends in 5 miles at the Rainbow Lakes Campground. The road is closed in winter and is good for ski touring.

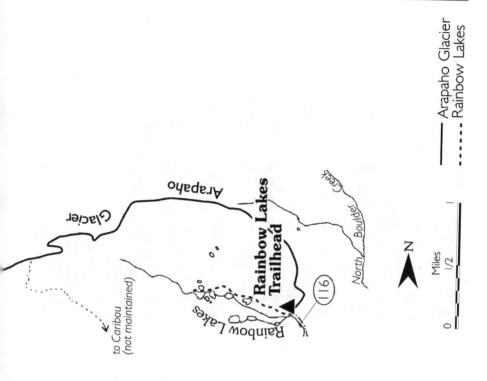

Arapaho Glacier Trail to Arapaho Glacier Overlook

(See map on page 154 and above)

Distance: 6 miles one way
Elevation: 9,920 to 12,720 feet
Highlights: Views of glacier, peaks, plains and lakes, alpine wildflowers
Difficulty: Strenuous
Topo map: Ward, Monarch Lake

Description

The Arapaho Glacier Trail, formerly called the "Glacier Rim Trail," skirts Boulder's watershed (closed to the public) and climbs to the glacier overlook. The best views of the lush, forbidden basin that contains Albion, Goose, and Silver Lakes (part of the watershed closure) are seen from this trail.

Starting at the Arapaho Glacier Trailhead in a mixed coniferous forest, just before a wilderness boundary sign, the trail passes through the last outposts of twisted limber pine and into the tundra after about 2 miles. A

Rainbow Lakes in fog

barbed wire fence in the forest and frequent no-trespassing signs above timberline separate the watershed from Forest Service land. Ignoring these signs can result in a $100 fine, and rumors circulate that University of Colorado runners have been hired to catch trespassers.

At timberline, you can look down into the Rainbow Lakes and the Boulder watershed lakes. The plains stretch out to the east, and the Arapaho peaks loom ahead. The higher you climb, the better the views become. The trail circles below a 10,000-foot-plus knob and climbs the north-facing slope of Arapaho Ridge, eventually crossing the ridge to the south-facing slope. From the south side there are views down into Diamond Lake and across to Mounts Evans, James, Grays, and Torreys. On a clear day you can see Pikes Peak, far to the south.

Early in the season snowfields may cover parts of the trail at this point, but cairns show the way to go. About a mile from the overlook, a faint, unmarked route descends a shallow valley on the left to the Caribou townsite (see **Bald Mountain,** page 157).

At the glacier overlook, views in every direction are superb, except for a Boulder watershed sign right in front of the glacier view. Sliding down the glacier, a popular sport in the old days, is forbidden.

History

The watershed has been closed to the public since 1920. The first Civilian Conservation Corps camp in Boulder County was established in the Nederland area in 1933. CCC men rebuilt the road from Silver Lake to Albion Lake and fenced in the watershed. In 1934 CCC workers from a seasonal camp at Peaceful Valley built 45 miles of trail in the Indian Peaks area in addition to forest improvement projects, fire fighting, and road and dam building.

Connections

If one party parks at Rainbow Lakes Campground and another at Buckingham Campground (sometimes called "Fourth of July Campground"), each party can make a 10-mile, one-way hike on the Arapaho Glacier and **Arapaho Pass** trails by arranging for a key exchange at some point along the way (see **Arapaho Pass Trail** on page 161). It's also possible to climb South Arapaho Peak from the overlook.

The **Rainbow Lakes Trail** (see page 153) also begins at the Rainbow Lakes Campground.

Access

From the Peak-to-Peak Highway (SR 72) halfway between Nederland and Ward, turn west onto CR 116 at the University of Colorado Mountain Research Station sign. This rough, gravel road dead-ends in 5 miles at the Rainbow Lakes Campground. The road closes at the research station turn-off during winter and is good for ski touring.

CARIBOU AREA

Our favorite thing to do in this historic area is to wander, with no particular destination, and look at ruins and wildflowers. Most of the area is part of Roosevelt National Forest, but some private inholdings and working mines are closed to the public. Many intersecting jeep roads make good hiking routes, but there are no officially maintained or marked trails.

Bald Mountain

Distance: Approximately 4 miles one way
Elevation: 10,000 to 11,340 feet

Highlights: Views of Indian Peaks, alpine wildflowers
Difficulty: Strenuous
Topo map: Nederland

Description

Bald Mountain is a stony lump on Arapaho Ridge. The ridge extends due east from South Arapaho Peak and is visible from Arapahoe Avenue in Boulder. Bald Mountain itself is not spectacular, but the views from it are, and it can be climbed earlier in the season than many other peaks. The unmarked route includes segments of several old roads and some cross-country hiking—it should be avoided by hikers who prefer well-defined trails, as it is easy to get off course. We once climbed all the way to Arapaho Glacier by mistake when we neglected to bring a map.

Starting on FS jeep road 505, the route goes past the ruins of an old log cabin and climbs the hill to the south. It drops gently through a limber pine forest and then levels out. When you come to a fork, take the right branch and go west past two tarns on your left, with Caribou Hill on your right. This road climbs to a saddle and branches again. You can either take the right branch, which drops to join another jeep road that meanders up the valley, or, to avoid losing altitude, you can contour cross-country across the flanks of Klondike Mountain and join the road higher up (a topo map is very useful here). Turn left onto this road and continue up to a second saddle northwest of Klondike Mountain. From this saddle, the road turns right (northwest) and quickly narrows to a trail, which ascends steeply up the ridge. The hill immediately above this second saddle is not Bald Mountain, but an unnamed bump on the ridge leading to Bald Mountain. Near treeline, the trail becomes indistinct and is marked by cairns.

Soon after you reach the tundra, a Forest Service sign marks the wilderness boundary. Ahead are spectacular views of the Indian Peaks. The pointed top of South Arapaho Peak is especially dramatic. Not so dramatic is your destination, Bald Mountain, the talus-covered hump to the right of and much lower than South Arapaho Peak. At this point, you should leave the cairned trail, which continues up the valley to join the Arapaho Glacier Trail. Contour up the grassy slope to the right of the trail, heading toward Bald Mountain. A final talus-scramble leads to the summit, marked by a cairn. The view includes Pikes Peak to the far south, Mount Evans and James Peak to the south, and the Indian Peaks to the west and northwest. Diamond Lake lies in the valley to the southwest. The Forest Service may post signs in the future discouraging use of this area.

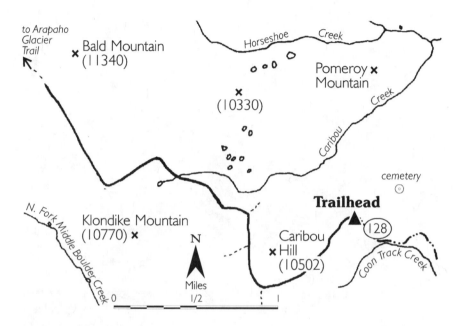

Bald Mountain

History

Silver was discovered in Caribou in 1869, and by the following year more than thirty-five mines were in operation. Over the years, more than $20 million worth of silver was taken from these mines. In 1872, a solid silver brick walk from the main street of Central City to the Teller House was built from Caribou silver to welcome President Ulysses S. Grant.

During its heyday Caribou supported several hotels, saloons, and even a millinery and a photography studio. However, the town was a magnet for tragedy. Winters were hard and fires were frequent. Many children died from scarlet fever and diphtheria. Some families lost all of their children within the span of a week. After the catastrophic fire of 1879, the town began to die, and only a few foundations remain today. Even the cemetery has been nearly leveled by vandals.

The town may have been a magnet, quite literally, as it was built next to a "magnetic dike" that seems to attract electrical storms. In *A Look at*

View of South Arapaho Peak from the trail to Bald Mountain

Boulder, Phyllis Smith reports that when children wrote on the blackboard, static electricity gave them nasty shocks and that men wearing rubber boots became weak. Because of its exposed location, hikers should be especially wary of lightning around Caribou during the summer thunderstorm season.

Connections

To see the **Caribou Cemetery,** walk northeast uphill from the parking area. Climb **Caribou Hill** to see the nearby mining ruins via FS Road 505. Follow the road until it starts to drop, then turn right (west) and continue uphill. A benchmark gives the elevation (10,502 feet) at the summit. Note that many of the ruins are on private land. Please respect the rights of the landowners.

If you continue on the cairned route beyond the wilderness boundary sign mentioned in the description of this hike, you can join the **Arapaho Glacier Trail to Arapaho Glacier Overlook** (see page 155).

Access

Take CR 128 west from the Peak-to-Peak Highway (SR 72) just northwest of Nederland. The road is rough. Park at the top where the road branches in four different directions. Start your hike on FS 505.

ARAPAHO PEAKS AREA

Arapaho Pass, Fourth of July Mine, Dorothy Lake

(See map on page 163)

Distance: 3.3 miles one way
Elevation: 10,121 to 12,061 feet
Highlights: Spectacular views, wildflowers, alpine lakes, historic and prehistoric ruins
Difficulty: Strenuous
Topo map: Monarch Lake, East Portal

Description

An annual July trek to Arapaho Pass is a tradition with many Boulder hikers who pronounce the wildflowers there to be the best in the county. Blue columbine and scarlet paintbrush line the trail at mid-elevations; mertensia, mimulus, and monkshood mass along creek crossings; fields of yellow glacier lilies, uncommon on the east side of the Continental Divide, bloom at the edge of retreating snowfields; and alpine flowers carpet the tundra.

Starting in the spruce/fir forest at the Fourth of July Trailhead, the Arapaho Pass Trail crosses several small streams before fording a larger stream, which will probably wet your boots. If they don't get wet there, the tumbling creek you cross next will almost certainly wet your feet. A short distance beyond this crossing, 1.2 miles from the trailhead, the **Diamond Lake Trail** branches to the left and the Arapaho Pass Trail opens out into lush fields of flowers.

In 2.1 miles from the trailhead, you reach the site of the Fourth of July Mine. Here, the **Arapaho Glacier Trail** goes to the right and the Arapaho Pass Trail contours up to the pass, following the route of an old wagon road. Pikas and marmots usually squeak and whistle along this section of the trail, which is quite stony and crosses snowfields early in the season.

At the pass (elev. 11,906 feet) you can look west/northwest down into Caribou Lake and Coyote Park, or seek shelter from the wind behind prehistoric hunting blinds. The 0.5-mile trail to Dorothy Lake, one of the deepest and coldest lakes in the region, goes up to the left of the pass.

History

The flat area around the Fourth of July Mine was one of the largest hunting camps on the Front Range, dating as far back as the Paleo-Indians. The area was used most recently by Ute and Arapaho tribes. Archaeologist Jim Benedict has identified several hunting blinds and game drive walls on the pass. He has directed excavations (done by volunteers from the Colorado Archaeological Society) at the mine and at Caribou Lake, uncovering ancient steam pits and charcoal used to boil roots. Benedict says that this pass was the only important prehistoric travel route across the Continental Divide between Devils Thumb Pass and Buchanan Pass.

A wagon road crossed over "the savage rim of Arapahoe Pass" late in the 1800s. In 1904, the state appropriated $5,000 to build a road, but only the east side was completed. And in the 1960s, a toll road was proposed and defeated.

Silver was discovered in the area in 1875 by C. C. Alvord. He established the Fourth of July Mine.

Connections

Both the **Diamond Lake Trail** (see page 166) and the **Arapaho Glacier Trail** (see page 164) branch off from the Arapaho Pass Trail. At

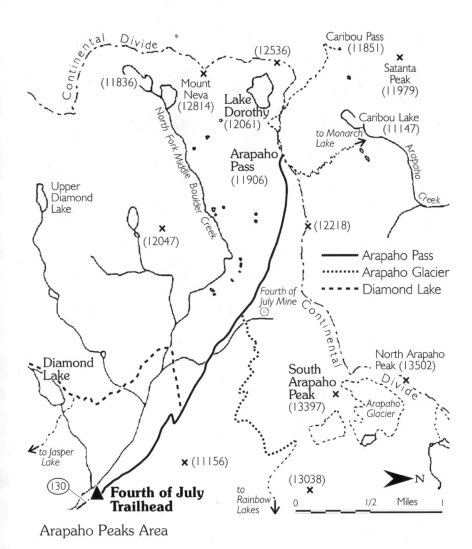

Arapaho Peaks Area

the pass, the Arapaho Pass Trail drops down to **Caribou Lake** and follows Arapaho Creek down to **Monarch Lake,** making a good backpacking route. The **Caribou Trail** continues above Dorothy Lake and leads over **Caribou Pass,** offering good views of **Columbine Lake.** A snowfield across Caribou Pass persists until mid-summer, and the trail is in bad shape with narrow and exposed stretches.

*Fourth of July Mine, at the intersection of Arapaho Pass and
Arapaho Glacier Trails*

Access

From the southwest end of Nederland, take CR 130 (off of SR 72) past
the town of Eldora to the Hessie junction. Take the right branch for another
4 miles to Buckingham Campground (also called Fourth of July Campground). At the campground, take the right fork up to the parking lot at the
Fourth of July Trailhead.

Arapaho Glacier Trail to South Arapaho Peak

(See map on page 163)

Distance: Approximately 4 miles one way
Elevation: 10,121 to 13,397 feet
Highlights: Spectacular views, wildflowers, glacier
Difficulty: Strenuous
Topo map: Monarch Lake, East Portal

Description

Arapaho Glacier—the largest glacier in Colorado—is one of the primary sources of Boulder's water. In fact, Boulder is the only city in the United States to own a glacier. During the Pleistocene, the glacier may have been 10 to 15 miles long and 1,000 feet deep. Today, it is 0.5-mile square and 200 feet deep.

Starting at the Fourth of July Trailhead, follow the **Arapaho Pass Trail** across a number of creek crossings to the Fourth of July Mine (see page 161 for details on this stretch of the hike). At the trail junction, the Arapaho Glacier Trail branches to the right and the Arapaho Pass Trail contours up to the pass.

Follow the glacier trail to the right, marked with cairns, around the south-facing shoulder of South Arapaho Peak and onto the tundra. About halfway up there are good views of Diamond Lake and peaks to the south. A large rock shelter at the overlook protects hikers from the usually fierce wind and provides a good lunch spot. A very large marmot lives nearby. The glacier itself is an immense expanse of snow, which terminates in a small turquoise pool far below.

Cairns on the south-facing side of the peak indicate the best route up the talus to the top of South Arapaho Peak (elev. 13,397 feet). Strong, experienced climbers can continue another 0.75 mile along the ridge to North Arapaho Peak (elev. 13,502 feet). Note that there is some exposure here.

History

In 1897, botanists Darwin M. Andrews (for whom Boulder's Arboretum is named) and Herbert N. Wheeler of the U. S. Forest Service were botanizing on the east side of Arapaho Pass, looking for dogtooth violet bulbs (glacier lilies). They hiked across what Boulderites then called "the big snowbank" and recognized it as a true glacier, which they reported to the University of Colorado. On July 14, 1900, Eben G. Fine, early Boulder druggist and outdoorsman, made a solo ascent of South Arapaho Peak and also found the glacier, which he publicized widely.

Possibly the first settlers to climb the Arapaho Peaks were three prospectors (W. C. Andree and two unnamed Hungarians) who climbed one of the peaks in 1861, thinking it was Longs Peak.

City Engineer Fred Fair developed much of Boulder's watershed beginning in 1904 and was one of the early promoters of tourism in the Indian Peaks area. For many years, Fair and the Boulder Chamber of Commerce championed the idea of a road to the glacier overlook and received an initial appropriation from Congress. Fair was even given a concessioner's permit to build shelters and refreshment stands at the overlook. As a publicity stunt, the Denver and Interurban Railroad in 1923 offered $1,000 to any aviator who landed a plane on the St. Vrain Glacier, which provided a smoother landing field than Arapaho Glacier. Charles Lindbergh accepted the challenge. However, the offer was withdrawn when Fair considered the unfavorable publicity that would ensue if Lindbergh happened to crash.

Fortunately, the road to the glacier was never built, and in 1927 the City of Boulder bought 3,685 acres of watershed, including the glacier, from the federal government for $4,606.

From 1938 to 1974, the Boulder Chamber of Commerce sponsored an annual August hike up to the glacier. Forty-eight people made the hike in 1938, growing to 600 in 1974. Too many people and heavy environmental damage brought these megahikes to an end.

Connections

Connecting trails are: **Arapaho Pass** (see page 161), which branches off at the Fourth of July Mine and continues to the pass; **Diamond Lake** (see page 166), which branches off between Buckingham Campground and the Fourth of July Mine; and the section of **Arapaho Glacier Trail** (see page 155) that continues east downhill to Rainbow Lakes Campground.

Access

From the southwest end of Nederland, take CR 130 off of SR 72 past the town of Eldora to the Hessie junction. Take the right-hand branch another 4 miles to Buckingham Campground (also called Fourth of July Campground). At the campground, take the right fork up to the parking lot at the Fourth of July Trailhead.

Diamond Lake

(See map on page 163)

Distance: 2.6 miles one way
Elevation: 10,121 to 10,960 feet
Highlights: Alpine lake, waterfalls, wildflowers, shady coniferous forest
Difficulty: Moderate
Topo map: Monarch Lake, East Portal

Description

Diamond Lake lies almost at timberline. It is reached via a trail that passes through a variety of habitats offering a wonderful display of wildflowers. It's a trail that will especially delight bog aficionados as it passes numerous marshy areas filled with bog orchids and other flowers that like wet feet. Hikers can keep their feet dry (mostly) thanks to boardwalks across the wettest areas.

Starting at the Fourth of July Trailhead, follow the Arapaho Pass Trail for 1 mile, across a number of stream and creek crossings, to the junction with the Diamond Lake Trail, which veers to the left (see page 161 for details on this first stretch of the trail). The tumultuous cataract on the opposite side of the valley flows from Diamond Lake.

Go left on the Diamond Lake Trail. You drop about 240 feet to the North Fork of Middle Boulder Creek, crossing several small streams en route. Cross the creek on the double log bridge (a vast improvement over the old log crossing) and follow the trail up through a spruce/fir forest with several small stream crossings. Snow persists on this section of the trail long after it has melted elsewhere. Just before you reach the lake, the forest opens out into a large, marshy meadow filled with flowers in summer. Between the meadow and the lake, a trail junction sign points to the left for **Devils Thumb Trail** and **Jasper Lake.** Continue straight ahead for Diamond Lake, and on a sunny day you will see how it got its name.

The trail continues on the right-hand side of the lake to two inlets at the upper end. It's worth climbing the trail beside the first inlet creek to a willow bog for the view of the braided cascade that originates at Upper Diamond Lake. From here, faint trails (not maintained by the Forest Service) lead to Upper Diamond Lake and to a tarn old-timers call "Banana Lake" because of its shape. These lakes, high in an alpine basin, are beautiful, but reaching them involves some cross-country hiking, so a topo map is useful if you decide to go. The route we prefer crosses the first inlet stream and proceeds on the right-hand side of the second stream up to "Banana Lake," which lies at the foot of a talus slope on the left-hand side of the basin. At the upper end of "Banana Lake," climb the rocky ridge to your right, cross to the right-hand side of the basin, and follow the small stream up past a terminal moraine to Upper Diamond Lake, which lies in a dramatic glacial cirque.

Connections

Devils Thumb Bypass Trail (see page 174), leading to **Jasper Lake** and **Devils Thumb Pass,** branches to the left just before you reach Diamond Lake. By leaving one car at Hessie, you can make a one-way, one-day hike down, or you can continue up to **Jasper Lake** and **Rollins Pass** and down via the **King Lake Trail** (see page 176) for a spectacular two-day backpacking trip, ending up at Hessie.

Diamond Lake

At the junction with the **Arapaho Pass Trail** you can continue to the pass (see page 161) or to **Arapaho Glacier** (see page 164).

Access

From the southwest end of Nederland, take CR 130 off of SR 72 past the town of Eldora to the Hessie junction. Take the right branch for another 4 miles to the Buckingham (also called Fourth of July) Campground. At the campground, take the right fork up to the parking lot at the Fourth of July Trailhead.

HESSIE AREA

Hessie, a town founded in the 1890s by Captain J. H. Davis and named for his wife, was the largest mining camp in this area. Gold and silver mining was prominent throughout the region, especially at Lost Lake and around Jasper Creek, and ruins of mines and cabins are a fairly common sight.

Most of the trails described here go through moist coniferous forest with globeflowers, buttercups, and marsh marigolds blooming in early summer, and columbines, locoweed, and paintbrush a bit later. In autumn, the aspen groves around and above Hessie are worth visiting. In winter, the road into the townsite and beyond makes a good ski tour, as does the road up to Buckingham Campground.

Lost Lake

(See map on page 170)

Distance: 1.4 miles one way
Elevation: 9,000 to 9,800 feet
Highlights: Waterfalls, turbulent creek, lake, mountain views
Difficulty: Easy
Topo map: Nederland

Description

From the townsite of Hessie, which is privately owned with some cabins still occupied, take the old jeep road up to the bridge across the North Fork of Middle Boulder Creek. Cross the bridge and continue up the main road, which is closed to motorized vehicles at the bridge. The road zigzags a couple of times up through aspen groves and a meadow as it climbs a ridge. When you hear the roar of a waterfall, take a short detour to your left to see one of the best waterfalls in the county. Dippers nest behind these falls in June, and a rainbow is usually visible in the morning.

Beyond the falls, the road continues to a trail junction sign at another bridge, which crosses the South Fork of Middle Boulder Creek. The **Devils Thumb Bypass Trail** goes up the right-hand side of the creek. Ignore this trail, cross the bridge, and continue up the left-hand side of the creek past another tumultuous waterfall. In spring, the section of the trail beyond these falls flows with snowmelt and is almost a creek itself. I once caught a fish in the middle of the trail with my bare hands and released it back into the "real" creek.

The trail continues uphill to Woodland Flats, where it opens up with views of Devils Thumb and the surrounding mountains. The view is so splendid that it's easy to miss the trail sign pointing left for Lost Lake, another 0.5 mile up from the flats.

A walk around the lake is pleasant, but beware of avalanche danger on the west side in winter. The views to the north are especially good and,

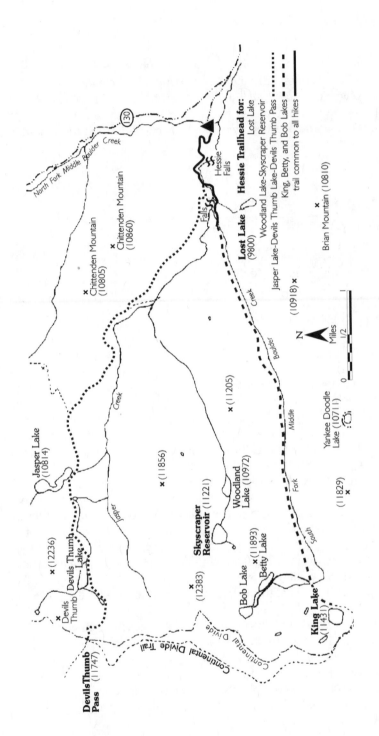

Hessie Area

Waterfalls near Hessie

across the lake to the west, mine tailings and the ruins of a cabin can be seen.

An old alternate route down via the south side of Middle Boulder Creek has been closed because the bridge on private property is no longer safe.

History

Approximately 200 people once lived and mined around this lake during the summer months.

Connections

At the second bridge, the **Devils Thumb Bypass Trail** leads to Jasper Lake, Devils Thumb Lake, and Devils Thumb Pass (see page 174). At Woodland Flats, you can continue on the **King Lake Trail** that heads west, following the creek up to King, Betty, and Bob Lakes and Rollins Pass (see page 176), or on the **Woodland Lake Trail** to Woodland Lake and Skyscraper Reservoir (see next trail description).

Access

Take CR 130 past the town of Eldora (west of Nederland and north of the Eldora ski area) to the sign for Hessie, 1.5 miles beyond Eldora. The rough gravel road to Hessie drops to the left. To reach the Hessie parking area, you must drive through water that may be fairly deep in spring. Four-wheel-drive and high clearance vehicles are helpful. If you decide to hike rather than drive this last bit of road, a bypass hiking trail leads around the wet section. Don't park along sections of the road that are posted with "No Parking" signs. Fines are stiff and cars have been towed away.

Woodland Lake, Skyscraper Reservoir

(See map on page 170)

Distance: 4.3 miles one way to Woodland Lake, 4.8 miles to Skyscraper Reservoir
Elevation: 9,000 to 10,972 feet at Woodland Lake to 11,221 feet at Skyscraper Reservoir
Highlights: Waterfalls, turbulent creek, lakes, mountain views
Difficulty: Strenuous
Topo map: Nederland, East Portal

Description

From the townsite of Hessie, take the old jeep road up to Woodland Flats, crossing both the North Fork and the South Fork of Middle Boulder Creek. (See Lost Lake Trail, page 169, for more details on this section of the hike.) At the sign for the **Lost Lake Trail,** which veers to the left, continue straight ahead for a short distance to a bridge across the South Fork of Middle Boulder Creek. Just beyond the bridge, the trail forks again with the left branch leading to **King Lake.** Again, continue straight ahead on the Woodland Lake Trail past the Indian Peaks Wilderness Boundary sign and through a meadow filled with wildflowers in summer (this is the same as the original **Devils Thumb Pass Trail).** This section of the trail also passes by old beaver ponds and through some marshy areas where bog orchids and little-red-elephants bloom profusely.

In about a mile the trail makes another fork, with the right branch going to **Jasper Lake** and **Devils Thumb Pass,** and the left fork to Woodland and Skyscraper Lakes. At this point, it's worth stopping at the small waterfall below the bridge over Jasper Creek to look for dippers (water ouzels). Continue up the Woodland Lake Trail, climbing steeply on the left side of the creek (a tributary of Jasper Creek) that drains Woodland Lake. After the trail crosses the creek (no bridge), it makes a wide sweep to the right and eventually returns to parallel the creek up through a spruce/fir forest to Woodland Lake.

The trail continues on the right-hand side of the lake and climbs steeply for about a half-mile up the remnants of an old road to Skyscraper Reservoir. This last segment of the trail is somewhat faint and may be covered by snowfields early in the season. If you lose the trail, stay high on the right-hand side of the valley, avoiding the boggy area near the creek that flows out of the reservoir.

History

Everett Long (whose family started Long's Iris Gardens on North Broadway in 1905) built Skyscraper Reservoir for irrigation between 1941 and 1947. He sold the reservoir and water rights to the City of Boulder in 1966.

Connections

Trails to the following destinations all start from the Hessie townsite and can be connected with the Woodland Lake Trail: **Lost Lake** (see page 169), **King Lake** (see page 176), and **Jasper Lake** and **Devils Thumb Pass** (see page 174). You can make a nice loop by returning from Woodland Lake via the Devils Thumb Bypass Trail, which can be picked up just beyond the bridge over Jasper Creek.

Access

Take CR 130 past the town of Eldora (west of Nederland and north of the Eldora ski area) to the sign for Hessie, 1.5 miles beyond Eldora. The rough gravel road to Hessie drops to the left. To reach the Hessie parking area, you must drive through water that may be fairly deep in spring. Four-wheel-drive and high clearance vehicles are helpful. If you decide to hike rather than drive this last bit of road, a bypass hiking trail leads around the wet section. Don't park along sections of the road that are posted with "No Parking" signs. Fines are stiff and cars have been towed away.

Jasper Lake

Jasper Lake, Devils Thumb Lake, Devils Thumb Pass

(See map on page 170)

Distance: 4.5 miles to Jasper Lake, 5.5 miles to Devils Thumb Lake, and 7.1 miles to Devils Thumb Pass one way
Elevation: 9,000 to 10,814 feet at Jasper Lake, to 11,160 feet at Devils Thumb Lake, to 11,747 feet at Devils Thumb Pass
Highlights: Waterfalls, cascading creeks, lakes, views, tundra, wildflowers
Difficulty: Strenuous
Topo map: Nederland, East Portal

Description

The basin below Devils Thumb, the prominent gendarme visible from many spots in the Hessie area, is dotted with lakes and tarns, including Jasper Lake, nestled into the spruce/fir forest, and Devils Thumb Lake, which lies at timberline at the very base of Devils Thumb.

From the townsite of Hessie, take the old jeep road up to the bridge across the North Fork of Middle Boulder Creek. Cross the bridge and continue to the trail junction sign at the bridge that crosses the South Fork of Middle Boulder Creek. For details on this first stretch of the trail, see the description for Lost Lake (page 169).

At the bridge, two routes to Jasper Lake and Devils Thumb Pass diverge. The original Devils Thumb Pass Trail crosses the bridge, follows the road up to Woodland Flats, and crosses the South Fork of Middle Boulder Creek a second time. It then continues along the west side of Jasper creek to a bridge and rejoins the Devils Thumb Bypass Trail on the east side of the bridge across Jasper Creek.

However, we prefer the Devils Thumb Bypass Trail because it is a real trail, not an old road, and is a bit shorter and less swampy. For the Bypass Trail, do not cross the bridge. Take the Devils Thumb Bypass Trail up the right-hand side of the creek through a moist coniferous forest that opens out into a flower-filled meadow below Chittenden Mountain. About half a mile beyond the Indian Peaks Wilderness Boundary sign, the Devils Thumb Bypass Trail rejoins the other fork of Devils Thumb Trail that comes in from the left. Although there are no signs, a left turn onto this road takes you across Jasper Creek and connects to a trail that leads up to Woodland Lake and Skyscraper Reservoir. This fork is also an alternate route back to Hessie.

To reach Jasper Lake, continue uphill, staying on the right-hand side of Jasper Creek for about 2 miles. You can either follow the road, which is straightforward but stony and hard on the feet, or you can take a trail, which crisscrosses the road a few times and is marked with cairns. Partway up this trail, a faint, cairned trail forks to the right and leads to Diamond Lake. Several old road remnants may cause some confusion, but these are usually closed off with logs or branches.

At the ruins of an old log cabin, the trail forks. Both forks cross Jasper Creek on logs just below Jasper Lake. An attractive waterfall flows across a logjam at the outlet of the lake, another waterfall cascades into the upper end, and a rock rib creates the illusion that there are two lakes.

The trail skirts the lower end of Jasper Lake and climbs on to Devils Thumb Lake in another mile, passing several tarns along the way. The best view of Devils Thumb is from the outlet of Devils Thumb Lake. The trail crosses the creek at the outlet and skirts the southern edge of the lake. It climbs past a grassy tarn and then zigzags steeply up to the pass.

A corniced snowfield on the trail to the pass lasts until late in the season and, in some years, it never melts. You can sometimes detour around it or follow the footsteps of other hikers up and across the snow. This snow-field may be impassable for inexperienced hikers during some seasons.

From the pass, marked by a massive cairn, the views in all directions are superb, especially to the north and west where the Never Summer and the Gore mountain ranges dominate the skyline.

Connections

Follow the ridge south to pick up the **High Lonesome Trail,** a segment of the **Continental Divide National Scenic Trail,** which leads to **Rollins Pass** and is marked with cairns. This trail crosses the tundra at about 12,000 feet on the west side of an east-facing escarpment, below a jagged ridge. If the weather is good, we prefer to follow the ridge, looking down into the lake basins to the east. Shortly before reaching Rollins Pass, there are views of **King, Bob,** and **Betty Lakes** framed in the pinnacles of the ridge. A good two-day backpacking loop can be made by following the **Continental Divide National Scenic Trail** south to Rollins Pass, and returning via the **King Lake Trail** (see below). This loop offers several miles of alpine gardens for flower enthusiasts as well as possible sightings of ptarmigan and elk.

A hard-to-find trail to **Diamond Lake** (see page 166) branches to the right a short distance below Jasper Lake. Trails to **Lost Lake** (see page 169) and to **Woodland Lake** and **Skyscraper Reservoir** (see page 172) also start from the Hessie townsite and can connect with the Devils Thumb Trail.

Access

Take CR 130 past the town of Eldora (west of Nederland and north of the Eldora ski area) to the sign for Hessie, 1.5 miles beyond Eldora. The rough gravel road to Hessie drops to the left. To reach the Hessie parking area, you must drive through water that may be fairly deep in spring. Four-wheel-drive and high clearance vehicles are helpful. If you decide to hike rather than drive this last bit of road, a bypass hiking trail leads around the wet section. Don't park along sections of the road that are posted with "No Parking" signs. Fines are stiff and cars have been towed away.

King, Betty, and Bob Lakes

(See map on page 170)

Distance: 5.2 miles one way to King Lake, with a 0.5-mile spur to Betty and Bob Lakes

Betty Lake

Elevation: 9,000 to 11,431 feet at King Lake, to 11,440 feet at Betty Lake, to 11,600 feet at Bob Lake
Highlights: Waterfalls, turbulent creek, lakes, mountain views, alpine flowers
Difficulty: Strenuous
Topo map: Nederland, East Portal

Description

From the townsite of Hessie, take the old jeep road up to Woodland Flats, crossing both the North Fork and the South Fork of Middle Boulder Creek. See the Lost Lake Trail description, page 169, for scenic details on this section of the hike. At the sign for the Lost Lake Trail, which veers to the left, continue straight ahead for a short distance to another bridge across the South Fork of Middle Boulder Creek. Just beyond the bridge, the trail forks again with the right fork going to **Woodland Lake, Jasper Lake,** and **Devils Thumb Lake** and **Pass.** Take the left fork (the King Lake Trail), which parallels the creek through coniferous forest and meadows. At the upper end of the valley, the trail zigzags steeply up a headwall to cross the creek. There's no bridge, but you can either jump or use stepping stones.

Just before this creek crossing, at 11,200 feet, a "user trail" (a trail not officially maintained by the Forest Service) branches to the right. A sign, now missing, formerly marked this junction. At present, the trail is obscure and may be hard to find; a topographic map would be very helpful.

Follow the faint trail marked by cairns up a ridge through krummholz, willow, and alpine flowers to Betty Lake. From the ridge, look south for views of the old Moffat Railway and the Devils Slide Trestles. The trail continues along the left-hand side of Betty Lake, crosses the outlet creek, and climbs a lateral moraine to Bob Lake, a beautiful glacial lake fed by a small waterfall. Between these two lakes the trail virtually disappears but is marked by occasional cairns. Stay well to the left of the creek flowing out from Bob Lake.

Descend via this same route (an elevation loss of about 400 feet) back to the King Lake Trail that climbs on up to King Lake, nestled in a glacial cirque.

Connections

Trails to the following destinations all start from the Hessie townsite and can be connected with the King Lake Trail: **Lost Lake** (see page 169), **Jasper Lake** and **Devils Thumb Pass** (see page 174), and **Woodland Lake** and **Skyscraper Reservoir** (see page 172). A good, two-day backpacking loop can be made by continuing on the King Lake Trail up to the **Continental Divide National Scenic Trail.** Continue north to connect with the **Devils Thumb Trail,** which comes up a side ridge south of Devils Thumb Pass. Complete the loop via **Devils Thumb Bypass Trail.** Use a topographic map for this loop as some of the connections may not be obvious. This loop offers miles of alpine gardens for flower enthusiasts. Watch for marmots, ptarmigan, pika, and pipits on the tundra.

Access

Take CR 130 past the town of Eldora (west of Nederland and north of the Eldora ski area) to the sign for Hessie, 1.5 miles beyond Eldora. The rough gravel road to Hessie drops to the left. To reach the Hessie parking area, you must drive through water that may be fairly deep in spring. Four-wheel-drive and high clearance vehicles are helpful. If you decide to hike rather than drive this last bit of road, a bypass hiking trail leads around the wet section. Don't park along sections of the road that are posted with "No Parking" signs. Fines are stiff and cars have been towed away.

EAST PORTAL AREA

Although most of this area lies in Gilpin County, we're including it because it's just barely over the county line, and it includes especially beautiful lakes, trails, wildflowers, and views. Traditionally, several of the trails described here have started at the East Portal of the Moffat Tunnel. This trail hub was open to the public for many years by permission of three generations of the conservation-minded Toll family who owned much of the land in the area. Early in 1994, the Wilderness Land Trust bought 1,320 acres and held it in trust until the U.S. Forest Service could obtain funds from Congress to buy it. In November, 1994, the land was purchased by the Forest Service and added to the Roosevelt National Forest. The Forest Service emphasizes backcountry non-motorized recreation in this area, and Congress may designate it as wilderness in the future.

We have described alternative trails to popular destinations in the James Peak area. Most of these trails are actually easier than starting from the East Portal of the Moffat Tunnel. Signs giving mileage will probably be installed at East Portal in the future. A network of trails from this point already exists and is shown on topographic maps.

History

Because all the trails in this section have historic ties to Rollins Pass and the railroad, we'll start with a general history of the area.

The route over Rollins Pass was first used by Native Americans, and stone hunting blinds and game drive walls can still be seen in various places. John Fremont's party crossed the pass in the 1840s and left two men buried at Deadman's Gulch, now part of the Eldora Ski Area. The first road over the Continental Divide into Middle Park was opened in 1866 by General John Q. Rollins, who improved an old army route and ran it as a toll road. Rollins also established the town of Rollinsville and refused to allow saloons, gambling, or dance halls within the city limits.

David H. Moffat built his famous railroad across the pass in 1903. Railway workers called the townsite at the summit "Corona—The Crown of the

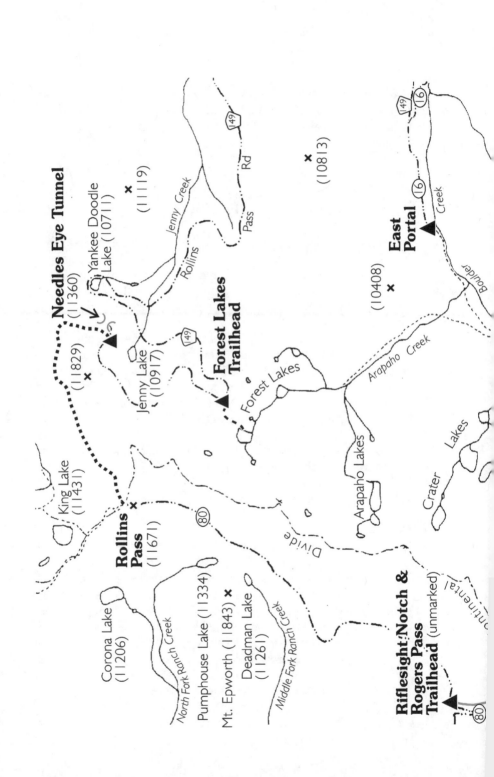

Needles Eye Tunnel

Yankee Doodle
Lake (10711)

✕
(11119)

Jenny Creek

Rollins

Pass Rd

✕
(10813)

✕
(11360)

✕
(11829)

King Lake
(11431)

Jenny Lake
(10917)

149

**Forest Lakes
Trailhead**

Forest Lakes

✕
(10408)

**East
Portal**

49
16

16

Creek

Boulder

Arapaho Creek

**Rollins
Pass**
(11671)

✕
(11671)

80

Corona Lake
(11206)

North Fork Ranch Creek

Pumphouse Lake (11334)

Mt. Epworth (11843) ✕

Deadman Lake
(11261)

Middle Fork Ranch Creek

Arapaho Lakes

Crater   Lakes

Divide

**Riflesight Notch &
Rogers Pass
Trailhead** (unmarked)

Continental

80

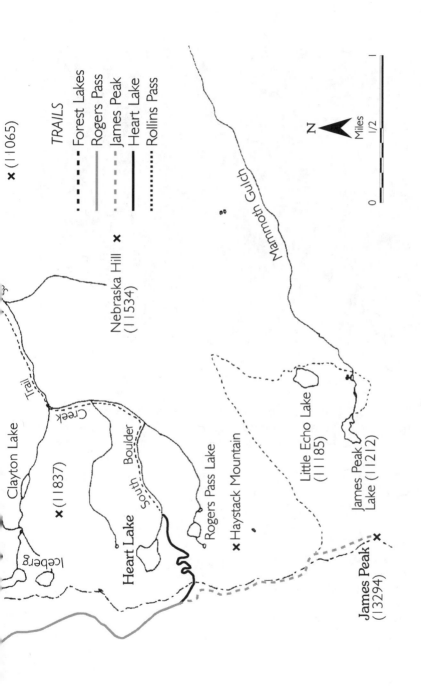

TRAILS

- ▪▪▪ Forest Lakes
- —— Rogers Pass
- ----- James Peak
- —— Heart Lake
- ····· Rollins Pass

✕ (11065)

Nebraska Hill ✕
(11534)

Clayton Lake

✕ (11837)

Iceberg

Heart Lake

Clayton
Creek
Trail

South Boulder Creek

Rogers Pass Lake

✕ Haystack Mountain

Little Echo Lake
(11185)

James Peak
Lake (11212)

James Peak ✕
(13294)

Mammoth Gulch

N

Miles
0   1/2   1

East Portal Area

Hikers making their way down to the Forest Lakes

Top of the World." It was the highest railroad station in the world. A railroad station, hotel, and restaurant thrived here until 1928, when Moffat Tunnel was completed and the line over the pass was closed. You can still see rail ties, remnants of the old snowsheds that protected the trains from avalanches, and some building foundations at the top of the pass. Although the pass is officially known as Rollins Pass, many of us still call it "Corona Pass."

Forest Lakes
(See map on pages 180–181)

Distance: 0.5 mile one way (to the first lake)
Elevation: 11,000 to 10,680 feet
Highlights: Lake surrounded by sheer cliffs, moist coniferous forest, array of wildflowers
Difficulty: Easy
Topo Map: East Portal

Description

From the ridge above Rollins Pass, we have counted eight lakes and tarns in the Forest Lakes basin, ranging from alpine glacial tarns to large, heavily wooded lakes, and ranging in color from turquoise to near-black. However, most of these can be reached only by rough fishing trails. The two largest lakes are reached by Forest Service Trail 809, a very good, well-defined trail starting at the Forest Lakes Trailhead. This trail is different from most because you reach the lakes by going down.

The trail drops from the Rollins Pass Road to the main lake in about half a mile. A rough trail circles the lake. We recommend taking this long route, turning right at the lake and circling beneath the dramatic cliffs and gendarmes and below a cascade bordered with wildflowers. At the lake's outlet, another fishing trail leads down the east side of the creek, past another small lake, to the lower Forest Lakes.

As you circumnavigate a large bog near the lower of the two largest lakes, look to the west side for the remains of a small red-and-white plane that crashed here many years ago. Mushrooms and wildflowers are especially profuse in this area—and so are bogs.

This route is shorter and easier than the route starting from the East Portal of Moffat Tunnel.

Connections

If you decide to start at the East Portal of Moffat Tunnel, hike about 1 mile west from the railroad tracks (at the end of the road) to a large meadow where two trails diverge. The left trail climbs steeply to **Heart Lake** (3.5 miles), the right trail (not quite as steep) leads to the lowest Forest Lake in about 4 miles. Beyond the meadow, the Forest Lakes Trail follows an old road for awhile, but the route is not marked and is very easy to lose once the road peters out. The trail also fords several rushing creeks without benefit of bridges. However, it's an excellent ski touring trail in winter.

A short distance beyond the Forest Lakes parking area, the road is closed to both vehicle and foot traffic at the Needles Eye Tunnel. However, if you walk the faint trail above the tunnel you can continue up the ridge through tundra wildflowers and look down into the Forest Lakes. If you ascend this ridge, look for Native American game drive walls and blinds.

It's also possible to cross above the tunnel, drop back down onto the road, and follow it as far as the Devils Slide Trestles, marked as unsafe by Forest Service signs.

Access

From Boulder, take SR 119 to Rollinsville. Turn west onto CR 16. In 7.5 miles, the road forks, with the left fork leading to the East Portal of Moffat Tunnel. Continue right on the Rollins Pass Road for another 11 miles. The road gets fairly rough, passing Yankee Doodle and Jenny Lakes en route. The parking area for Forest Lakes is on a hairpin curve just above Jenny Lake.

James Peak via Rogers Pass Trail

(See map on pages 180–181)

Distance: 3.5 miles one way
Elevation: 11,000 to 13,294 feet
Highlights: Spectacular views, tundra flowers
Difficulty: Strenuous
Topo map: East Portal, Empire

Description

The views from a "thirteener" are almost as spectacular as from a "fourteener," and the climb is a bit easier. From James Peak, the prominent mountain visible from many points in Boulder County, you can see all the way from Pikes Peak in the south to Longs Peak in the north. Some additional "fourteeners" seen from the summit include Mounts Evans and Bierstadt, Grays Peak, Torreys Mountain, and Mount of the Holy Cross.

Starting in the spruce/fir forest at the Rogers Pass Trailhead at Riflesight Notch, the trail (actually an old road) contours gently up the hill toward Rogers Pass at 11,860 feet. Shortly after you reach timberline, another old road comes in from the left. (If you just want a wildflower walk, this is a pleasant road to explore.) At about 1.5 miles you cross an old ditch, and soon the **Continental Divide National Scenic Trail** (marked by massive cairns as well as white posts with blue insignia) joins the Rogers Pass Trail from the left.

Continue for a short distance on this merged trail, but don't go all the way to Rogers Pass. Just before Rogers Pass, the Continental Divide Trail drops slightly to the right and contours around Haystack Mountain before climbing to a slight saddle below the summit ridge of James Peak. Look for an ancient Native American hunting blind and a game drive wall on this

James Peak

saddle. The Continental Divide Trail continues to follow the divide south all the way to Berthoud Pass and beyond. At the saddle, leave the Continental Divide Trail and follow the large stone cairns straight up the talus slope to the summit.

History

Dr. Edwin James, a member of Major Stephen H. Long's expedition, was the first man on record to climb a 14,000-foot peak in the United States. He and two companions climbed Pikes Peak (which Pike never climbed) in 1820. Long, in the early 1820s, was probably the first white explorer to enter Boulder County. Later, James Peak was named for Edwin James and Longs Peak for Stephen Long.

The trestle at Riflesight Notch was part of the "Loop" on David Moffat's railroad line. At this point, the train crossed the notch on the trestle, circled the hill, went through a tunnel (now collapsed) beneath the trestle, and descended to Middle Park. See page 179 for additional information on Rollins Pass and the railroad.

Connections

From Rogers Pass, you can drop 1 mile down on the **South Boulder Creek Trail** (a continuation of Rogers Pass Trail) to **Heart Lake** (see next trail description) or continue in either direction on the **Continental Divide National Scenic Trail** for seemingly limitless tundra walking.

Access

From US 40, take the Rollins Pass turnoff (CR 80) across from the Winter Park Ski Area and drive 12 miles up to the Rogers Pass Trailhead, which begins on the right-hand side of the road across from the trestle over Riflesight Notch. Park in wide spots along the road.

James Peak can also be climbed from St. Mary's Glacier. For this route, take I-70 past Idaho Springs and turn right at the St. Mary's Glacier turnoff.

A third, much longer trail (a segment of the South Boulder Creek Trail) starts at the East Portal of Moffat Tunnel and climbs past Heart Lake to Rogers Pass. For this route, take SR 119 from Boulder to Rollinsville and turn west onto CR 149. In 7.5 miles, the road forks, with the right fork continuing on the Rollins Pass Road. Take the left fork, which leads to the East Portal of Moffat Tunnel.

Heart Lake

Heart Lake via Rogers Pass Trail

(See map on pages 180–181)

Distance: 3 miles one way
Elevation: 11,000 to 11,860 feet at Rogers Pass, and down to 11,320 feet at Heart Lake
Highlights: Spectacular views, alpine flowers, alpine lake
Difficulty: Moderate
Topo map: East Portal

Description

From Riflesight Notch, take the Rogers Pass Trail to Rogers Pass. Shortly after you reach timberline, an old road comes in from the left, and just before you reach Rogers Pass, the **Continental Divide National Scenic Trail** merges with the Rogers Pass Trail for a short distance (see page 184 for a more detailed description). From the pass, the trail (now called the **South Boulder Creek Trail**) zigzags down to aptly named Heart Lake, which nestles in the curve of a glacial cirque at timberline. Some krummholz borders the lower end of the lake. Heart Lake lies to the left of the trail, and Rogers Pass Lake (not quite as beautiful as Heart Lake) is to the right.

Connections

This lake can also be reached by following the **South Boulder Creek Trail** up 5 miles from East Portal. From this trail, a faint side trail leads to **Crater Lakes,** and a very rough route goes to **Clayton** and **Iceberg Lakes.**

From Rogers Pass, you can climb **James Peak** (see page 184) or connect with the **Continental Divide National Scenic Trail.**

Access

From U.S. 40, take the Rollins Pass turnoff (CR 80) across from the Winter Park Ski Area and drive 12 miles up to the Rogers Pass Trailhead, which begins on the right-hand side of the road, across from the trestle over Riflesight Notch. Park in wide spots along the road.

Rollins Pass Road from Needles Eye Tunnel to Rollins Pass

(See map on pages 180–181)

Distance: 1.5 miles one way
Elevation: 11,360 to 11,671 feet
Highlights: Spectacular views, alpine flowers, historic ruins
Difficulty: Easy
Topo map: East Portal, Empire

Description

From the Needles Eye Tunnel, which has been closed for safety reasons, walk up a faint trail starting on the left-hand side of the tunnel. On

Rock Shelter above Needles Eye Tunnel on Rollins Pass Road

King Lake

top of the tunnel are the remains of several old stone structures that were probably connected with the railroad. If you take a detour (no trail) to the top of the ridge, you may see ancient Native American hunting blinds and game drive walls.

Continue walking west across the tundra to the jeep road that drops down from Rollins Pass. You can hike this road up to the pass, or you can follow the old railroad bed below, which was formerly the continuation of CR 149 and is now closed to vehicular traffic.

The railroad route crosses two railroad trestles that are marked unsafe. You'll have to decide for yourself whether to heed this warning. Views down into **Betty** and **King Lakes** and across to a braided waterfall are beautiful, and the wildflowers and alpine butterflies along the edges of this railroad route are especially good. Continue on up to Rollins Pass at the Continental Divide and enjoy the magnificent views.

Connections

From Rollins Pass just north of the parking area you can drop down to the **King Lake Trail** (see page 176) or continue on the **Continental Divide National Scenic Trail** in either direction.

Access

From Boulder, take SR 119 to Rollinsville and turn west onto CR 149. In 7.5 miles the road forks, with the left fork leading to the East Portal of Moffat Tunnel. Turn right on the Rollins Pass Road and continue for 11 miles to the road closure, south of Needles Eye Tunnel. Park in wide spots along the road.

Nearby State and County Parks

Several state parks and a Jefferson County park are close to Boulder and offer excellent hiking trails. The trails described here are our favorites.

ELDORADO CANYON STATE PARK

Rattlesnake Gulch

Distance: 1.5 miles one way (to hotel ruins)
Elevation: 6,050 to 6,760 feet
Highlights: Views of red rock formations and rock climbers, hotel ruins, woodland and canyon birds
Difficulty: Moderate
Topo map: Eldorado Springs

Description

At the Rattlesnake Gulch Trailhead sign, follow the trail to your left and enjoy views of the red rock walls that form a spectacular gateway to Eldorado Canyon. At the first switchback, the **Fowler Trail** goes behind the Bastille rock formation to the eastern park boundary. Part of this section is the grading for an old railroad, the Colorado-Utah-Southern Company. Started in the late nineteenth century to compete with the Moffat Railroad, which was built about 1,500 feet higher, this company ran into the hard rock of the Bastille as well as financial problems. The railroad was never completed beyond this point. Along the way you'll find a bench where you can sit to watch rock climbers.

From the switchback, the main trail climbs to a flat area below an aqueduct. It then drops down to cross a small stream, which may be dry in summer.

From the aqueduct the trail zigzags up an east-facing slope to the ruins of The Crags Hotel. This hotel, which could once reached by train from above

Rattlesnake Gulch

or by tramway from the canyon bottom, opened in 1908 and shortly thereafter burned down in 1912. Only the foundations, a fireplace, and the basin of an ornamental fountain remain. Junipers, Douglas-firs, and ponderosa pines now grow out of the crumbled brick and crockery shards while sumac thrives in the fountain.

At the south (upper) end of the ruins plateau, the trail forks, making a 2.2-mile loop up to the Santa Fe and Rio Grande Railroad at 7,220 feet.

If you time your hike to coincide with the schedule of the train, you can watch it emerge from one tunnel and enter another one. Amtrak usually passes through in late morning. We prefer to go up the right branch of this loop because it is shadier and descend via the sunny left-hand trail. A short distance up the right branch a spur goes to a viewpoint for the Continental Divide.

History

Eldorado Springs has been famous for its thermal waters and resorts since the early 1900s, when a 100-room hotel with two ballrooms and three swimming pools was built along the creek. This resort was so popular that the Denver and Interurban Electric Railway ran a spur line to it, and the Eisenhowers honeymooned here.

The canyon is also famous because of Ivy Baldwin who walked a 7/8-inch cable strung between the Bastille and Wind Tower at a height of 685 feet. He crossed the high wire eighty-nine times starting in 1906, sometimes performing stunts such as standing on his head or pretending to fall. He made his final, successful crossing on a lower wire in 1948 on his eighty-second birthday.

In 1978 two parcels of Eldorado Canyon (Inner Canyon and Crescent Meadows) were purchased for the state park that is internationally renowned for its rock climbing.

Connections

Near the park entrance, the **Streamside Trail** goes along the north side of South Boulder Creek, giving access to various rock climbing routes such as the Wind Tower and Redgarden Wall. When traffic is light, it's pleasant to walk through the park along the road itself, with splendid views down into the pools and rapids of South Boulder Creek. The road ends in a picnic area just beyond the bridge at the upper end of the park. From this point you can take the **Eldorado Canyon Trail,** approximately 4 miles, to Walker Ranch (see page 112).

Access

Turn west from U.S. 93, 4 miles south of Boulder, onto Eldorado Springs Drive and continue to the west end of town. A state parks pass is required for all park visitors beyond the sign. Walk or drive 0.6 mile up the road to a small parking area at the Rattlesnake Gulch Trailhead.

Views of the Bastille and Eldorado Resort from the Crags Hotel ruins

WHITE RANCH PARK (JEFFERSON COUNTY)

White Ranch Park in Jefferson County covers 3,040 acres and includes 18 miles of multi-use trails. Two of our favorite hikes are described here. To sort out the many intersecting trails, be sure to get a map at the west parking lot. The rock formations throughout the park are rich in mica, and many of the trails glitter like gold because of this mineral.

Rawhide Loop

Distance: 4.5 miles round trip
Elevation: 7,500 feet, with losses and gains of several hundred feet
Highlights: Views of Denver and the plains, wildlife, wildflowers, historic farm equipment
Difficulty: Easy to moderate
Topo map: Ralston Buttes, Golden

Description

We like to start at the west end of this loop, which follows an old ranch road downhill in a northerly direction. The trail goes up and down through open meadows and ponderosa pine forests. At 1.1 miles, the **Wrangler's Run Trail** forks to the right, and at the Sourdough Springs Equestrian Camp the **Waterhole Trail** also forks to the right. Both of these trails reconnect with the Rawhide Trail making shorter loops possible.

In about 2.5 miles the Rawhide Trail turns east, narrows, and begins the return part of the loop through Douglas-fir and ponderosa pine trees, with views of the Ralston Buttes and of Denver. This section is especially lovely in late April and early May when the pink-flowering cacti are blooming and the blue grouse are booming.

Just before reaching the parking lot, you pass through an "open air museum" with interpretive signs, featuring nineteenth-century harrows, seed drills, and other farming machinery.

History

The Paul White family homesteaded part of this land and ran a cattle ranch here in the early 1900s.

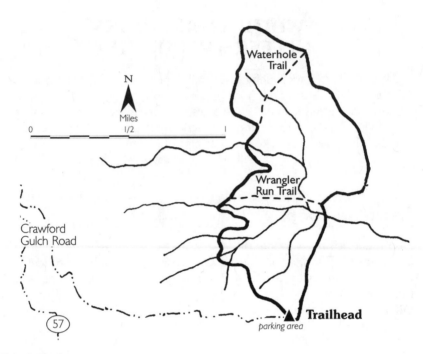

Rawhide Loop

Access

Take SR 93 south from Boulder and turn west on CR 70 (Golden Gate Canyon Road), 0.5 mile before reaching Golden. Continue 4 miles. Turn right on CR 57 (Crawford Gulch Road) and follow the signs for White Ranch Park. Park at the second parking lot.

Belcher and Mustang Trails

Distance: 4.7 miles one way
Elevation: 7,500 to 8,000 to 6,150 feet
Highlights: Views of rock formations, cliffs, canyon, wildflowers
Difficulty: Moderate
Topo maps: Ralston Buttes, Golden

Old manure spreader at White Ranch Farm

Description

If you leave one car at the lower parking area and another at the upper lot, these trails can be combined for a one-way hike, mostly downhill, that passes through numerous life zones. Actually, several intersecting trails in this area can be combined for various loops and permutations, but the Belcher-Mustang combination gives especially good views of cliffs and a deep canyon formed by Van Bibber Creek.

Starting in ponderosa pines, the Belcher trail climbs Belcher Hill (elev. 8,000 feet), the highest point in the park. At 0.3 mile, just before reaching the hilltop, Mustang Trail branches to the right and descends along an intermittent stream. (If you wish to climb Belcher Hill, make a short detour and then return to the Mustang Trail.)

After leaving the stream, the trail heads east, going up and down across several arroyos to rejoin the Belcher Hill Trail, which continues downhill along an old road to the lower parking lot. The final 2 miles of the trail cross rolling grasslands that are filled with wildflowers in the spring, but which can be very hot.

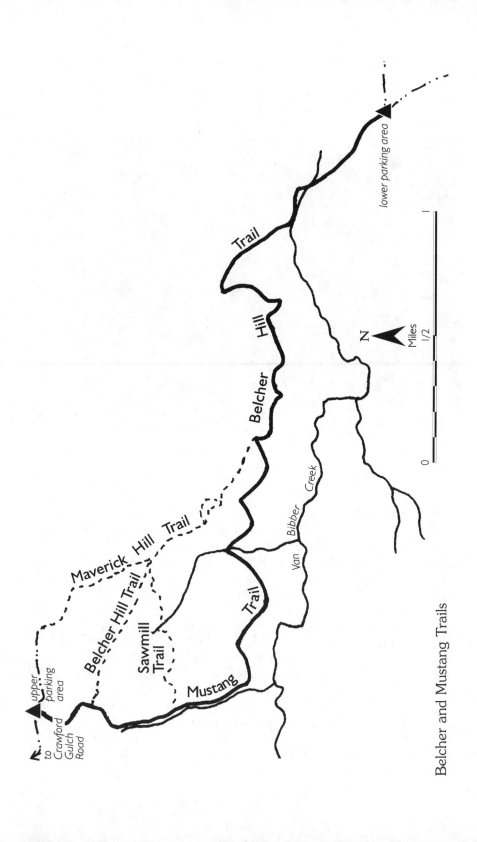

Belcher and Mustang Trails

Access

The lower parking lot is 1 mile west of SR 93. Turn right (west) off of SR 93 on West 56th Street about half a mile before reaching Golden, and follow the White Ranch Park signs. To reach the upper parking lot at the west end of White Ranch Park, turn west on CR 70 (Golden Gate Canyon Road) off of SR 93, 0.5 mile before reaching Golden. Continue 4 miles. Turn right on CR 57 (Crawford Gulch Road) and follow signs for White Ranch Park. Park at the second parking lot.

GOLDEN GATE CANYON STATE PARK

More than 35 miles of trails crisscross this state park, which is one of our favorite places for early spring flowers and for autumn aspen. Many of the trails, labeled with signs depicting wildlife tracks, eventually lead to Frazer Meadow, a grassy opening surrounded by aspen and containing the ruins of an old homestead. Our favorite trail is the next one described.

Frazer Meadow Trail

Distance: 1.8 miles one way
Elevation: 8,200 to 9,200 feet
Highlights: Aspen, wildflowers, grassy meadows
Difficulty: Easy
Map: Park map available at Visitor Center

Description

Autumn aficionados will delight in this trail, which passes through aspen groves and an understory of shrubs and herbaceous plants that turn scarlet, crimson, and gold in September.

Starting at the Frazer Meadow Trailhead, the trail (designated by a horseshoe symbol on the signs) parallels a small seasonal stream, crossing it several times. At the first fork, the right-hand trail goes to **Greenfield Meadows** and some backcountry camp sites. Continue on the left-hand branch, which crosses and then leaves the stream. The trail climbs up past the **Ground Squirrel Trail** and merges with the **Mule Deer Trail.** At the Mule Deer intersection, turn right, cross the stream, and stop at the

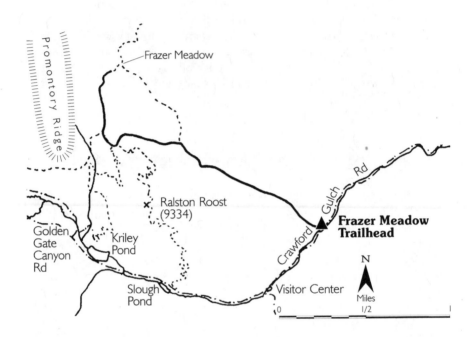

Frazer Meadow Trail

historic ruins. Aspen circle the meadow, and beyond the aspen, a coniferous forest cloaks craggy rock formations.

History

John Frazer homesteaded here in 1880 and raised hay, which he handcut with a scythe. He was noted for never sleeping in a bed, preferring ground or floor.

Much of the present-day state park was once famous for its bootlegging—an operation commemorated by the place-name "Bootleg Bottom." As many as seventeen stills may have been active in the 1920s, when local farmers were the principal suppliers for Denver and Central City. The chief entrepreneur and his driver transported the whisky (made from

Aspen line the trail to Frazer Meadow

corn, sugar, water, and yeast) and gin (flavored with juniper berries) in a wagon labeled "Smith's Breadwagon." They always flipped a coin to decide what route to take and ran cattle behind the wagon to obliterate the tracks.

One of the early settlers in the area was Anders Tallman who proved up his homestead in 1882. He chose the area around present-day Forgotten Valley because the timber reminded him of his native Sweden.

Connections

So many trails interconnect in this park that hikers can make almost endless permutations, looping in whatever direction fancy takes. By doing a car shuttle, you can hike from one end of the park to the other, from Bootleg Bottom to the Frazer Meadow Trailhead, for instance. Check the park map for possibilities.

Access

Take SR 93 south from Boulder to Golden Gate Canyon Road (CR 70). Turn west and continue for about 14 miles to the Visitor Center, where a map and a required state parks pass can be obtained. Frazer Meadow Trailhead is about half a mile east of the Golden Gate Canyon State Park visitor center, on the north side of the road.

BARR LAKE STATE PARK
Gazebo Trail

Distance: 1.5 miles one way
Elevation: About 5,150 feet, with no elevation gain
Highlights: Birdwatching, nature study, lake and mountain views
Difficulty: Easy
Map: Barr Lake (Colorado State Parks)

Description

The Nature Center should be your first stop after obtaining the state parks pass. There are good displays, and a bulletin board lists recently observed species of birds and mammals. Park naturalists often give guided walks and can tell you what to look for.

From the south parking lot and picnic area, cross the bridge over the Denver and Hudson Canal and turn left (south). Almost immediately, you

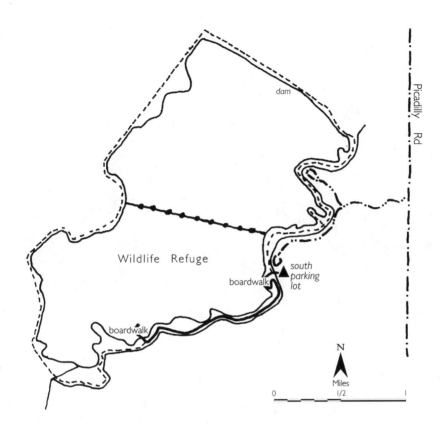

Gazebo Trail

have a choice: the left branch stays high, whereas the right branch takes a short detour on a boardwalk out over the water. If you're birdwatching, take the boardwalk!

The boardwalk soon rejoins the main trail, which follows the lakeshore around to another boardwalk leading out to a gazebo usually equipped with a viewing scope. From here you can watch a rookery populated by great blue herons and cormorants. For several years a pair of bald eagles has nested in the vicinity of this rookery and can often be seen in April and May, along with white pelicans, western grebes, and various other waterbirds. From May until fall migration, warblers, orioles, and other colorful birds can be seen in the cottonwoods along the shoreline. Over

Bald eagle's nest at Barr Lake State Park

330 species of birds have been seen in the park, which serves as the headquarters for the Colorado Bird Observatory, a nonprofit organization for research on western birds.

History

This 1,918-acre reservoir dates back to the late 1880s and was a popular fishing lake, in addition to providing water storage and irrigation. From the 1940s through the 1960s, pollution from nearby Denver sometimes created rafts of whitish, soapy-looking bubbles that were more common than rafts of white pelicans. However, a new sewage treatment plant improved the water quality, and Barr Lake was opened as a state park in 1977. The southern half of the lake is now a wildlife refuge, and the northern half is open to boating and fishing.

Connections

A 9-mile, unnamed trail, including the segment described previously, circles the entire lake.

Access

From Boulder, take SR 7 to Brighton. Just before reaching Brighton, turn right onto US 85. In a few blocks, turn left onto Bromley Lane. Continue east on Bromley Lane to Picadilly Road. From here, large brown signs direct you to Barr Lake, which is located at 13401 Picadilly Road. Stop at the entrance for the required state parks pass and for a brochure and map. For more information on activities at Barr Lake State Park, call (303) 659-6005.

Appendices

A. BEST OF THE BEST FOR . . .

Aspen viewing: Frazer Meadow Trail or any Golden Gate Canyon State Park trail (see page 201); lower portions of Hessie area trails (see page 168–179); Switzerland Trail, west from the Sugarloaf parking area (see page 56)

Sumac, autumnal shrubs, and fall flowers: Bluebell-Baird Trail (see page 88); Mesa Trail, south end (see page 84); Rattlesnake Gulch and Fowler Trail beyond the Bastille (see page 193)

Ski touring, mountains: Calypso Cascade Trail (see page 120); Buchanan Pass Trail (see page 128); Sourdough Trail (see page 147); Little Raven Trail (see page 151) and other Brainard area trails; Lost Lake and other Hessie area trails (see page 168); trails starting at the East Portal, Moffat Tunnel (see page 179)

Ski touring, foothills: Mesa Trail, north end (see page 84); McClintock and Enchanted Mesa Loop (see page 93); Meyers Homestead Trail (see page 116)

Ski touring, plains (only when there's a good snowfall): East Boulder Trails (see pages 16 and 18); Walden and Sawhill Ponds (see page 21); Coal Creek Trail (see page 37)

Birdwatching: Golden Ponds, part of St. Vrain Greenways Trail (see page 5); Coot Lake and Boulder Reservoir (see page 9); Sawhill and Walden Ponds (see page 21); East Boulder Trail, White Rocks Section (see page 16); Barr Lake State Park—usually a pair of bald eagles nest here (see page 204) (helpful hint: you meet the *nicest* people when using binoculars!)

People watching (and meeting people): Boulder Creek Path (see page 25); Mesa Trail (see page 84)

Early spring wildflowers (spring beauties, pasqueflowers, etc.): Rabbit Mountain (see page 46); Gregory Canyon (see page 77); Mesa Trail (see page 84) and any of its laterals; Hall Ranch (see page 49)

Late spring wildflowers (fairyslippers, clematis, etc.): Ceran St. Vrain (see page 137); Calypso Cascade (see page 120)

Summer wildflowers (too many to mention!): Arapaho Pass (see page 161); Diamond Lake (see page 166); Blue Lake (see page 142); Lake Isabelle (see page 143)

Tundra and alpine wildflowers: Mount Audubon (see page 139); Pawnee Pass (see page 143); Arapaho Pass (see page 161); South

Arapaho Peak (see page 164); Devils Thumb Pass (see page 174); James Peak (see page 184)

Prairie grasses: Big Bluestem (see page 102); East Boulder Trail, White Rocks Section (see page 16)

Waterfalls: Ouzel Lake via Calypso and Ouzel Falls (see page 120); Lost Lake (see page 169) or any of the trails starting in the Hessie area

Rock formations and interesting geology: Rabbit Mountain (see page 46); Red Rocks (see page 70); Hall Ranch (see page 49); Heil Ranch (see page 52); Mesa Trail (see page 84); First and Second Flatirons branches (see page 90)

Caves: Mallory Cave (see page 96)

Natural stone arch: Royal Arch (see page 90)

Glaciers: Gibraltar Lake, St. Vrain Glaciers (see page 123); Arapaho Glacier Trail (see pages 155 and 164); Isabelle Glacier Trail (see page 144)

Historical cabins and ranching artifacts: Betasso Preserve (see page 65); Towhee and Homestead Loop (see page 99); Meyers Homestead Trail (see page 116); Rawhide Loop (see page 197); Hall Ranch (see page 49); Heil Ranch (see page 52)

Narrow-gauge route and railroading artifacts: Rollins Pass Road (see page 188)

Indian game drive walls and blinds: Rollins Pass Road (see page 188); Arapahoe Pass (see page 161); James Peak (see page 184)

Weather interpretation: Walter Orr Roberts Nature Trail (see page 94)

Fishing: Ceran St. Vrain Trail along South St. Vrain Creek (see page 137); Rainbow Lakes (see page 153); Button Rock Preserve along North St. Vrain Creek (see page 43); Walker Ranch along South Boulder Creek (see page 112)

B. WHEELCHAIR-ACCESSIBLE TRAILS

This section is dedicated to Tom and Maddy Goldhawk for their courage and gallantry.

Most trails in the Boulder Greenways Program are wheelchair accessible. They are either paved or have a hard gravel or dirt surface. For a free Greenways Trails map, call (303) 441-3266. Another useful booklet, *Accessibility Guide to Eastern Boulder County Trails and Natural Sites,* including maps, is available for $10 at Boulder's Recreation Centers.

The following is a selected list of wheelchair-accessible trails described in greater detail earlier in this book:

- Boulder Creek Path (see page 25). This path is either paved or has a hard gravel surface for the entire distance.
- Centennial Trail (see page 31). The entire trail is paved.
- Coal Creek Trail (see page 37).
- Doudy Draw Trail (see page 110). The first 0.3 mile to a picnic area in a cottonwood grove is paved.
- Dry Creek Trail (see page 32).
- East Boulder Trail, Teller Farm Section (hard dirt) and Teller Lake No. 5 (see page 18).
- Gazebo Trail at Barr Lake State Park (see page 204). This level trail has a hard dirt surface.
- Long Lake (see page 143). This first segment of the Pawnee Pass Trail is dirt and would be feasible for wheelchairs only when dry. The grade is slightly steeper than six percent in places.
- Pella Crossing (see page 7).
- South Boulder Creek Trail (see page 30). The sections between Baseline and the East Boulder Community Center and between Valmont Lake and Arapahoe Road are paved. There is a nice loop around the lakes behind the East Boulder Community Center.
- St. Vrain Greenways Trail (see page 5). This Longmont trail is paved.
- Walden and Sawhill Ponds (see page 21). The network of paths through Walden are mostly of hard gravel. The Sawhill paths are mainly hard dirt.
- Walter Orr Roberts Nature Trail (see page 94). This path has a good gravel surface.
- Wonderland Lake (see page 62). This trail can be extended by taking paved walks through the Wonderland Hills neighborhood, such as the stretch from Wonderland Park to Kalmia and 4th Streets.

These short trails (most are less than 1 mile in length) are not described in this book:

- Bear Creek Trail. From the Reynolds Branch Library on Table Mesa Drive to its confluence with Boulder Creek, this trail is paved, and there are several branches going to different destinations.
- Bohn Park (in Lyons turn south on 2nd Street from US 36). This paved trail parallels the St. Vrain River from the park to SR 66 and provides excellent birdwatching. Another path heads east between the river and US 36.
- Cottonwood Park (Via Appia Way and South Boulder Road, Louisville). Sidewalks through this city park are paved.

- Heatherwood-Walden Trail (75th Street and Jay Road, Boulder). This trail is paved to the boundary with Walden Ponds.
- McIntosh Lake (Lakeshore Drive, Longmont). The sidewalk on the south shore is paved.
- Skunk Creek Trail (Vassar and Table Mesa Drives, Boulder). The first stretch of this trail is paved, becoming gravel as it dips down to Skunk Creek. The wheelchair-accessible portion ends at a small power station in a brushy area good for birdwatching. Stop to enjoy the serene wildlife paintings at the Moorhead and Martin underpasses. Another branch of this trail starts behind the National Institute of Standards and Technology (NIST) building (325 Broadway) and heads up the hill. From NIST a paved path also goes under Broadway to the BaseMar Center. It's worth a special trip to see the children's poetry and art that decorate this underpass.
- Tantra Park (46th Street and Hanover Avenue, Boulder). Several sidewalks through this park are paved.
- Viele Lake (South Boulder Recreation Center on Gillaspie Drive, Boulder). The sidewalk around the lake (wonderful for waterfowl watching) is paved and can be extended by taking the walk east of the Recreation Center.
- Waneka Lake Park (west end of West Emma Street or from Caria Drive, Lafayette). The path around the lake is mainly hard gravel with two paved sections. Mountain views and birdwatching are very good.

C. OUTDOOR ETHICS
(Adapted from the *Boulder County Nature Almanac*)

There's no shortage of hiking trails or outdoor places to go in Boulder County. But now there's also a superabundance of people, many of whom frequent these trails and places. To put things in perspective, according to naturalist Steve Jones, there are 250,000 humans and only a couple of dozen black bears; 110,000 human dwellings and only about 10 golden eagle nest sites; 60 retail florists and only a half-dozen known specimens of white adder's-mouth, one of our rarest orchids.

Whenever we go out into nature we run the risk of loving it to death. Although anyone who would use this book probably already "treads lightly" on the land, here are a few suggestions to help us all preserve the places we cherish.

- Leave wildflowers, plants, and even rocks for others to enjoy.
- Leave archaeological and historical artifacts undisturbed.
- Comply with signs regarding pets, and keep dogs leashed where required.
- Comply with signs regarding vehicles and mountain bikes, which are prohibited on many trails because of erosion problems.
- Do not shortcut trails. Shortcuts destroy vegetation and cause erosion.
- Build campfires only when and where they are permitted, and never leave one unattended.
- Bury human waste and bury or burn toilet paper.
- Leave gates open or closed, as they are found.
- Give right of way to horses, keeping to the downhill side. Horse riders should keep to trails.
- Do not disturb nesting birds, and comply with closures designed to protect plants or animals. Keep all pets out of these areas, too.
- When hiking on trails used for ski touring, avoid stepping in the ski tracks. Your steps can leave "post-holes" that can be dangerous for skiers.
- Do not leave trash or food behind. Carry out your litter and, if you want to do a good deed, carry out litter left by others.
- Respect no trespassing and private property signs. Explore only where you are permitted.

D. OUTDOOR SAFETY

(Adapted from the *Boulder County Nature Almanac*)

Taking precautions against hazardous conditions you may meet along any trail—from the plains to the mountains—can help make every hiking experience safe and pleasant. Here are a few tips on preparing for a safe hike in Boulder's outdoors.

- Dress appropriately for the weather, which can change quickly, especially in the mountains. Even in summer a light jacket and poncho may be needed. In winter, dress in layers for added insulation and to facilitate quick adjustments. Use a broad-brimmed hat or visor in summer and a warm cap in winter. Be aware of the symptoms of hypothermia.
- Use a sunscreen lotion with a rating of 15 or higher and wear dark, UV protecting glasses—Colorado's sun is fierce.
- Always take plenty of water, maps, emergency food, and basic first aid supplies, except for the easiest strolls.

- Don't hike alone. If you insist on going solo, be sure someone knows where you're going and when you'll return.
- Newcomers need time to acclimate to the high altitude. Be aware of the symptoms of altitude sickness. If you feel altitude sickness, return immediately to a lower elevation.
- In winter, be aware of avalanche danger and avoid areas where avalanches may occur.
- Anticipate thunderstorms on summer afternoons, especially at high elevations. If you are caught in a thunderstorm, get to a lower elevation quickly and avoid seeking shelter under isolated trees, rock formations, fences, and power lines. If lightning is actually striking around you, squat in the lowest area you can find.
- If a flood warning is issued, climb to the highest ground possible. Don't try to drive out of a canyon ahead of a flood.
- Don't drink water from lakes or streams. *Giardia lamblia,* a parasite that attacks the intestinal system, is widespread. Backpackers should treat water by boiling for 20 minutes or use a filter pump.
- Check for ticks, which can carry several diseases, during spring and summer. Brush them off if they have not yet embedded in your skin. If they are embedded, cover the tick with heavy oil and wait for half an hour. If it hasn't disengaged by then, use tweezers.
- Be extra careful around waterfalls, rushing streams, and irrigation ditches. Watch children in such circumstances.
- Be alert for such hazards as poison ivy, rattlesnakes, and mine openings and shafts.
- Do not eat mushrooms, berries, or plants unless you are absolutely positive of their identification.
- Be prudent around wildlife. Don't feed or pet wild animals, and don't come between a mother and her young. Although bear and mountain lion sightings are uncommon, they have been increasing in recent years. Back slowly away if a bear or mountain lion is sighted, avoid direct eye contact, and speak calmly. An attack is most unlikely. However, if a mountain lion stalks you, respond aggressively and make yourself appear as large as possible; don't run. If either a bear or lion attacks, fight back.

Bibliography

Maps
(Most of these maps are available at Boulder sporting goods and map stores or from the issuing agency.)

Boulder, Colo. Greenways Program. *Boulder Greenways: Self-Guided Tour Map*, 1999. Available free from the Boulder Greenways Coordinator, phone 441-3266.

Boulder, Colo. Open Space and Mountain Parks Lands. *Trails Map*, 1999.

Boulder County, Colo. Board of County Commissioners. *Boulder County Road Map*, 1999. Available from Boulder Chamber of Commerce, 2440 Pearl Street, Boulder, CO 80302.

Colorado Mountain Club, Boulder Group. *Ski Trail Map: Brainard Lake–Middle St. Vrain*, 1996.

Colorado Mountain Club, Boulder Group. *Trail Map: Boulder Mountain Parks and Nearby Open Space*, 1997.

Trails Illustrated Topo Maps: Indian Peaks, Gold Hill, Colorado. Evergreen, Colo.: Ponderosa Publishing Co., rev. 1996.

U.S. Forest Service. *Arapaho and Roosevelt National Forests*, 1997.

U.S. Geological Survey. *Boulder County, Colorado. 1:50,000-scale Topographic Map*, 1980.

U.S. Geological Survey. 7.5 minute series USGS topographic maps for smaller units, as noted in hike descriptions, various years.

Books
(Most of these books are available at the Carnegie or Boulder Public Libraries.)

Ament, Pat, and Cleve McCarty. *High Over Boulder*. Boulder, Colo.: March Press, 1976.

Arps, Louisa Ward, and Elinor Eppich Kingery. *High Country Names*. Boulder, Colo.: Johnson Publishing Co., 1972.

Benedict, James B. *Arapaho Pass*. Ward, Colo.: Center for Mountain Archaeology, 1985.

———. *Archaeology of the Coney Creek Valley*. Ward, Colo.: Center for Mountain Archaeology, 1990.

Bixby, Amos. "History of Boulder County." *History of Clear Creek and Boulder Valleys, Colorado.* Chicago: O. L. Baskin & Company, 1880.

City and County of Boulder. Miscellaneous city and county open space brochures. Boulder, Colo.: City and County of Boulder, various years. Available at Boulder Open Space offices and at trailheads.

Crossen, Forest. *Western Yesterdays: David Moffat's Hill Men.* Fort Collins, Colo.: Robinson Press, 1976.

Cushman, Ruth Carol, Stephen R. Jones, and Jim Knopf. *Boulder County Nature Almanac.* Boulder, Colo.: Pruett Publishing Co., 1993.

Eberhart, Perry. *Guide to the Colorado Ghost Towns and Mining Camps,* 4th ed. Chicago: Sage Press, 1969.

Exploring Boulder County, 2nd ed. Boulder, Colo.: Boulder County Parks and Open Space Department, 1993.

Folzenlogen, Darcy, and Robert Folzenlogen. *Walking the Denver-Boulder Region.* Littleton, Colo.: Willow Press, 1992.

Helmuth, Ed, and Gloria Helmuth. *The Passes of Colorado.* Boulder, Colo.: Pruett Publishing Co., 1994.

Hudson, Suzanne. *History of Boulder's Parks and Recreation, or How We Got to Be So Pretty.* Boulder, Colo.: Boulder Parks and Recreation Department, 1993.

Kenofer, Louis. *Rocky Mountain Trails.* Boulder, Colo.: Pruett Publishing Co., 1972.

Meier, Tom. *The Early Settlement of Boulder: Set in Type—Cast in Bronze—Fused in Porcelain.* "It Ain't Necessarily So." Boulder, Colo.: Boulder Creek Press, 1993.

Mitchell, Mark F. and Peter J. Gleichman. *Cultural Resource Inventory of the Contiguous Boulder Mountain Parks.* Unpublished manuscript, on file at City of Boulder Mountain Parks Department, 1996.

Murray, John A. *The Indian Peaks Wilderness Area: A Hiking and Field Guide.* Boulder, Colo.: Pruett Publishing Co., 1985.

Olmsted, Frederick Law. *The Improvement of Boulder County: Report to the City Improvement Association.* Boulder, Colo.: Boulder City Improvement Association, 1910.

Ormes, Robert M. *Guide to the Colorado Mountains,* 9th ed. Edited by Randy Jacobs. Denver, Colo.: Colorado Mountain Club, distributed by Cordillera Press, 1992.

Pettem, Silvia. *Boulder: Evolution of a City.* Niwot, Colo.: University of Colorado Press, 1994.

Roach, Gerry. *Colorado's Indian Peaks Wilderness Area: Classic Hikes and Climbs.* Golden, Colo.: Fulcrum Publishing Co., 1989.

——. *Flatirons Classics: A Guide to Easy Climbs and Trails in Boulder's Flatirons.* Golden, Colo.: Fulcrum Publishing Co., 1987.

Robertson, Janet. *The Front Rangers.* Boulder, Colo.: Colorado Mountain Club, 1971.

Schoolland, John. *Boulder in Perspective.* Boulder, Colo.: Johnson Publishing Co., 1980.

——. *Boulder Then and Now.* Boulder, Colo.: Pruett Publishing Co., 1979.

Smith, Phyllis. *A Look at Boulder: From Settlement to City.* Boulder, Colo.: Pruett Publishing Co., 1981.

Wolle, Muriel Sibell. *Stampede to Timberline.* Boulder, Colo.: Self-published, 1949.

Web Sites

www.fs.fed.us/arnf/districts/brd/hiking

www.ci.boulder.co.us/openspace/visitor/cherryvaletrail

www.ci.boulder.co.us/openspace/gis/netmap

www.co.boulder.co.us/openspace

Index

(Page numbers set in boldface type refer to major hike descriptions listed in the table of contents.)